FUNDAMENTALS OF PHARMACOVIGILANCE

A COMPLETE GUIDE FOR FRESHERS TO CRACK ANY TECHNICAL INTERVIEWS

SAUGATA GHOSH

Contents

Foreword

No drug which is pharmacologically effective is without hazard. Furthermore not all hazards can be known before a drug is marketed. Pharmacovigilance, which includes the procedures used to identify, evaluate, and minimise the hazards connected to medications in clinical use, is widely recognised as an essential component of public health. Most nations now have notification mechanisms in place for reporting information on adverse medication responses to the authorities as a direct result of the thalidomide catastrophe in the 1960s.

Since then, pharmacovigilance science, methodology, and technologies have developed, largely in response to the increasingly complicated drug safety challenges. Examples of this complexity include drug-related harms that may be difficult to separate from the ailment itself being treated, harms that may only become apparent after extremely long-term usage, and harms that may be similar to underlying pathologies in the population being treated.

These complex hazards necessitate the use of a variety of techniques and data sources together with solid judgement when applying them. It is now more suitable to discuss an integrated approach that may involve a variety of evidence rather than advancing up a ladder of evidence away from less reliable forms of data like single case adverse reaction reports.

Pharmacovigilance faces an equal or perhaps greater difficulty today than it did following the thalidomide tragedy. It is a challenge deserving of the dedication of all those engaged in the creation, marketing, and regulation of medications if the general public, patients, and healthcare professionals are to have confidence in the goods they use.

Dr. June Raine, Director of the Vigilance and Risk Management of Medicines Division, Medicines and Healthcare Products Regulatory Agency,London, UK and Chair of the EU Pharmacovigilance Working Party

Preface

Pharmacovigilance is the investigation of the efficacy of commercially available medications as they are used clinically in often sizable populations.

The effectiveness of the drug, whether it is used on healthy or ill individuals, the pharmaceutical quality of the drug, the nature and severity of any side effects and the extent to which these can be treated, the threat posed by the disease that is being treated with the drug, and the rest of the complex of issues that constitute holistic patient care must all be taken into account before safety can be considered.

Clinical drug safety, also known as pharmacovigilance, has seen a sharp increase in employment over the past ten years, particularly in the pharmaceutical sector. The trend appears to be continuing, hopefully indicating a greater emphasis on the security of medications. This book tries to give novices to the discipline, who by necessity are frequently narrowly focused, a quick and comprehensive introduction to the subject. My goal is to facilitate a quick knowledge of the environment and fundamental pharmacovigilance principles at the industry/regulatory interaction.

The newcomer must understand how we arrived to where we are right now.

I have started with the most significant Adverse effect and reaction because they have influenced the growth of pharmacovigilance. I'm hoping that the book will also make it clear to the newcomers that they are currently engaged in a fascinating and significant topic that is likely to see rapid growth in the foreseeable future.

I'm hoping the reader will want to keep reading instead of moving on. The reader should go on to the larger texts, where there are plenty of references, next. I've just identified a few key sources in the final chapter, but they are all significant and might be consulted for more reading.

Saugata Ghosh

Acknowledgements

Writing a book is harder than I thought and more rewarding than I could have ever imagined.

I'm eternally grateful to my mother Swapna Ghosh, who took in an extra mouth to feed when she didn't have to. She taught me discipline, tough love, manners, respect, and so much more that has helped me succeed in life. I truly have no idea where I'd be if she hadn't given me a roof over my head or became the guide whom I desperately needed at that age.

Prologue

The science and practises involved in the identification, evaluation, comprehension, and mitigation of side effects and other drug-related issues are referred to as pharmacovigilance.

This introduction is intended to help readers quickly grasp the fundamental ideas behind pharmacovigilance. It not only covers the techniques involved, but also the regulatory concerns, ethical, and societal considerations of pharmacovigilance. It is also jam-packed with cases showing drug safety issues.

This book is ideal for novices and required reading for students studying pharmaceutical medicine and those new to drug safety departments because it covers the fundamentals step-by-step.

ADE Adverse drug event/effect

ADR Adverse drug reaction

AEFI Adverse event following immunisation

AEMPS Agencia Española de Medicamentos y Productos Sanitarios *(Spanish Medicines and Healthcare Products Agency)*

ANSM Agence nationale de sécurité du médicament et des produits de santé, France *(has replaced AFSSAPS)*

API Active pharmaceutical ingredient (WHO)

ART Antiretroviral therapy

ARV Antiretrovirals

ATC Anatomical, Therapeutic, Chemical classification

BCPNN Bayesian Confidence Propagation Neural Network

BfArM Bundesinstitut für Arzneimittel und Medizinprodukte *(Federal Institute for Drugs and Medical Devices in Germany)*

BMA British Medical Association

CDC Centers for Disease Control and Prevention

CEM Cohort Event Monitoring

CIOMS Council for International Organizations of Medical Sciences

CRO Contract research organisation *(often responsible for clinical trials)*

DDD Defined Daily Dose

DIA Drug Information Association

DSRU Drug Safety Research Unit, Southampton, UK

DTC Direct to consumer

DTP Direct to patient

EEA European Economic Area

EMA European Medicines Agency

ENCePP European Network of Centres for Pharmacoepidemiology and Pharmacovigilance

EU European Union

E2B The current international standard for ADR reporting developed by ICH

FDA Food and Drug Administration *(USA regulatory body)*

FIC (WHO) Family of International Classifications

FIP International Pharmaceutical Federation

FOI Freedom of information

FTP File transfer protocol

GACVS Global Advisory Committee on Vaccine Safety (WHO)

GCP Good clinical practice.

GF Gates Foundation *(full name Bill and Melinda Gates Foundation)* or Global Fund *(see also GFTAM)*

GFATM Global Fund to Fight AIDS, Tuberculosis and Malaria

GLP Good laboratory practice

GMP Good manufacturing practice

GVSI WHO Global Vaccine Safety Initiative

GxP Generic term for good practice requirements in the pharmaceutical industry

HAI Health Action International

HATC Herbal ATC

HIC High income countries

HSA Health Sciences Authority, Singapore

IC Information Component (used in BCPNN) – Informed consent

ICD International Classification of Diseases

ICDRA International Conference for Drug Regulatory Authorities

ICH International Conference on Harmonisation of Technical Requirements for Registration of Pharmaceuticals for Human Use

ICSR Individual case safety report

IMB Irish Medicines Board

IMMP The Intensive Medicines Monitoring Programme, New Zealand

IMS Not an acronym. Company providing statistics and information in the health care sector

INN International non-proprietary names (*for pharmaceutical substances*)

IPCS International Programme on Chemical Safety

ISO International Organization for Standardization

ISoP International Society of Pharmacovigilance

ISPE International Society for Pharmacoepidemiology

JPMA Japan Pharmaceutical Manufacturer's Association

Lareb Netherlands Pharmacovigilance Foundation (*Landelijke Registratie en Evaluatie van Bijwerkingen*)

LMIC Low- and middle income countries

MAH Market authorisation holder

MedDRA Medical Dictionary for Drug Regulatory Affairs

MHRA Medicines and Healthcare products Regulatory Agency (UK)

MSH Management Sciences for Health

MSSO Maintenance and Support Services Organization (*for MedDRA*)

MSF Médecins Sans Frontières

NC National centre (for pharmacovigilance)

NCE New chemical entity

NDA New Drug Application

NGO Non-governmental organisation

NME New molecular entity

NRA National regulatory authority **NSAID** Non-steroidal anti-inflammatory drug **OTC** Over-the-counter

PCC Poison Control Centre

PDR Physician's Desk Reference

PDS Pharmacoepidemiology and Drug Safety (journal)

PEM Prescription event monitoring

PEPFAR US President's Emergency Plan for AIDS Relief

PHRMA Pharmaceutical Research and Manufacturers Association

PIL Package insert leaflet

PMDA Pharmaceuticals and Medical Devices Agency, Japan

PMS Post-marketing surveillance

POM Prescription only medicine

PPI Proton Pump Inhibitor

PRAC Pharmacovigilance Risk Assessment Committee (EMA)

PSM Procurement and supply management

PSUR Periodic safety update report

PV Pharmacovigilance

QA Quality Assurance

QSM-WHO Quality Assurance and Safety of Medicines (WHO)

RCA Root-cause analysis

SFDA State Food and Drug Administration, China

SMQ Standardized MedDRA Query

SOC System organ class

SOP Standard operating procedure

SPC Summary of product characteristics *(in the EU)*

SSFFC Substandard/Spurious/Falsely-Labelled/Falsified/Counterfeit (SSFFC) Medical Products (WHO)

SSRI Selective Serotonin Reuptake Inhibitor *(group of anti-depressants)*

TGA Therapeutic Goods Administration, Australia

THIN The Health Improvement Network, UK. A medical research database of anonymized patient records from general practitioners

TSR Targeted spontaneous reporting

UMC Uppsala Monitoring Centre

UNITAID *(Not an acronym)* Organization cooperating with WHO and others on the WHO millennium goals

VAERS Vaccine adverse event reporting system

WAHO West African Health Organization

WHO-ART WHO Adverse Reaction Terminology

WHO-CC WHO Collaborating Centre

WHO-DD WHO Drug Dictionary

WHO-DDE WHO Drug Dictionary Enhanced

XML Extensible Mark-up Language

Definition Used In Pharmacovigilance

ABUSE: Abuse is the intentional, non-therapeutic use by a patient or consumer of a product –over-the counter or prescription –for a perceived reward or desired non-therapeutic effect including, but not limited to, "getting high"(euphoria).

DRUG ADDICTION: Addiction is an overwhelming desire by a patient or consumer to take a drug for non-therapeutic purposes together with inability to control or stop its use despite harmful consequences.

MISUSE: Misuse is the intentional use for a therapeutic purpose by a patient or consumer of a product –over-the-counter or prescription –other than as prescribed or not in accordance with the authorisedproduct information.

COMPOUNDING: Compounding refers to products that are usually made by a pharmacist or physician.

DEVICE USE ERROR: An act or omission of an act that results in a different medical device response than intended by the manufacturer or expected by the operator.

DISPENSING ERRORS: Dispensing errors are not limited to pharmacists.It can include nurses and physicians.For example, physicians can dispense sample products in their office.

PRESCRIBING ERROR: Prescribing errors may be made in the hand of physicians or other healthcare professionals who have the prescription authority.

MEDICATION ERROR: Medication errors are defined as any preventable event that may cause or lead to inappropriate medication use or patient harm while the medication is in the control of the health care professional, patient or consumer. Such events may be related to professional practice, health care products, procedures and systems, including prescribing, order communication, product labeling, packaging and nomenclature, compounding, dispensing, distribution, administration, education, monitoring and use.

ADMINISTRATION ERROR: Any difference between what the patient received or was supposed to receive and what the prescriber intended in the original order.

OFF LABEL USE: Off label use relates to situations where a healthcare professional intentionally prescribes, dispenses, or recommends a product for a medical purpose not in accordance with the authorisedproduct information.

OVERDOSE: Overdose is more than the maximum recommended dose (in quantity and/or concentration), i.e., an excessive dose.

UNDERDOSE: Underdoseis the administration of less than the minimum recommended dose (in quantity and/or concentration).

OCCUPATIONAL EXPOSURE: Occupational exposure encompasses the "chronic" exposure to an agent (including therapeutic products) during the normal course of one's occupation, and could include additional scenarios in specific regulatory regions.

INTERCEPTED MEDICATION ERROR: Intercepted medication error refers to the situation where a medication error has occurred, but is prevented from reaching the patient or consumer.

INAPPROPRIATE SCHEDULE: Deviations from the prescribed dosage schedule.

PRODUCT QUALITY ISSUES: Product quality issues are abnormalities that may be introduced during the manufacturing/ labeling, packaging, shipping, handling or storage of the products.

LABELLED DRUG- DISEASE INTERACTION MEDICATION ERROR: This medication error refers to the situation when a patient is prescribed, dispensed, or administered a drug that is documented in the drug label as having the potential to exacerbate or worsen the patient's pre-existing disease(s).

LABELLEDDRUG-DRUGINTERACTION MEDICATION ERROR: This medication error refers to the situation when a patient is prescribed, dispensed, or administered a drug that is documented in the drug label to cause a drug to drug interaction with the patient's existing medication(s).

LABELLEDDRUG-FOOD INTERACTION MEDICATION ERROR: This medication error refers to the situation when a patient is prescribed, dispensed, or administered a drug that is documented in the drug label to cause an expected adverse event with patient's consumed food.

DRUG DIVERSION: Drug diversion means that a drug is diverted from legal and medically necessary uses toward illegal uses.

MEDICATION MONITORING ERROR: A medication monitoring error is an error that occurs in the process of monitoring the effect of the medication through clinical assessment and/or laboratory data. It can also refer to monitoring errors in following instructions or information pertinent to the safe use of the medication.

CHAPTER ONE

Adverse effect and reaction

Any undesirable or untoward reaction after taking a drug is kniown as adverse event.

No drugs are free of side effects. A drug can produce adverse effects and hence there always exists a risk. The amount of risk has to be considered along with the therapeutic benefit and if the benefit outweights the risk,the drug is administered to the patient.

The adverse reaction may develop immediately after taking a drug or even after a considerable amount of time; and even after the stoppage of the treatment. The effects may include a simple skin reaction to life-threatening conditions like myocardial infraction.

Overview

A **side effect** is any unintended effect after taking a drug. Although it is unintended but it colud be beneficial. Example: anxiolytic effect with beta-blocker. Such effects can be expected or unexpected; if unexpected then these are termed as **Unexpected Therapeutic Benefit (UTB).**

According to the WHO, an adverse medication reaction is a reaction that is harmful and unanticipated and that takes place at levels that are typically used in humans for the prevention, diagnosis, or treatment of illness or for the alteration of physiological function.

According toNew EU Pharmacovigilance Legislation, **Adverse drug reaction** is a noxious and unintended response to a medicinal product. This can be through the normal use of the medicine but also as a result of misuse, abuse or medication error, overdose, off-label use or during occupational exposure.

Adverse event can be defined as any untoward medical occurrence that can occur during treatment with a medicine, but it may or may not have a causal relationship with the treatment.

Thus the only point of difference between adverse drug reaction and adverse event is that the former has a causal relationship with the suspected drug whereas the later does not have such association with the drug. So all adverse drug reactions are adverse events but all adverse events are not adverse drug reactions.

DoTS Classification

Adverse drug reactions can be classified as per DoTS system. Do mean Dose, T stands for Time and S is Susceptibility.

DOSE

Toxic effects: Adverse effects that occurs at supratherapeutic dose or dose higher than therapeutic level.Ex- liver failure with high dose of paracetamol.

Collateral reactions include the reactions that occur at normal therapeutic doses.Ex- nausea with morphine.

Hypersusceptibility reactions: These reactions occur at subtherapeutic doses in susceptible individuals. Ex-Anaphylaxis with penicillin

TIME

Time-independent reactions: These reactions occur at any time during treatment and may be triggered by something which causes a change in drug concentration. Ex increase in warfarin dose increases haemorrhage risk.

Time-dependent reactions: These can be further classified into various categories.

Immediate reactions: These reactions occur when a drug is administered too rapidly)

First-dose reactions: They occur only after the first dose of treatment course.

Early reactions occur early in the course of treatment then abate with continuing treatment due to tolerance). Ex nitrate induced hedache.

Intermediate responses take some time to occur, but if they don't happen by a specific point, there is little to no risk. Exallegic reactions (ampicillin/amoxicillin pseudoallergic rash).

Late reactions: It includes withdrawal reactions that occur when, after prolonged treatment, a drug is withdrawn or its therapeutic dose is reduced. Ex paroxetine withdrawal syndrome.

*Delayed reactions*occur some time after administration and even if the drug is withdrawn before the reaction occurs. Ex clear cell cancer with stilbestrol.

SUSCEPTIBILITY

These reactions vary from person to person based upon different factors like Genetic variations, Age, Ethnicity, Altered physiology (pregnancy, weight), Gender, Disease and Exogenous factors.

Genetic variations: The study of the relationship between drug responsesand genome is known as pharmacogenomics.An individual's susceptibility to an adverse drug reaction is often determined by their genetic make-up. Example some people carry genetic alterations that reduce enzyme activity in the CYP2D6 gene as a result of which codeine is not converted to its active metabolite morphine.

Age: Children are more susceptible to a particular ADR compared to adultsYoung children may have an unexpectedly high bioavailability of a medicine, which raises the risk of ADRs.. Newborns and neonates have a large body surface area which increases permeability for compounds. Furthermore, the skin of children is thinner, sensitive and soft and can be easily damaged thus increasing absorption of substances applied to the skin.

Haemolysis occurs with chloroquine in G6PD deficiency as seen in children.

Gender: Women are 50 percent more likely than men to experience an adverse drug reaction. The hormonal effects, metabolism and immune system variations play a vital role.

Ethnicity: Research revealedthat Asians are at higher risk of anticoagulant-related ADEs. Black patients are frequently determined to be at higher risk for diabetes agents-related ADEs. Caucasiansare at increased risk for opioid-related ADEs.

Altered physiology: Pregnancy has an impact on drug treatment. Not only are women affected by the drug, but the fetus can also be exposed to ADRs of the drug. Drugs may permeate through the Blood Placental Barrier and may cause teratogenic effects. The thalidomide incident leading to phocomelia is an example of such teratogenicity. Morphine Sulfate Injection USP causes more severe adverse effects including respiratory depression in women.Obese people may store large amounts of fat-soluble drug as they have higher amount of fatty tissues, whereas very thin people may store relatively little.

Disease state: The pathological state of body causes significant effect in drug action. Various diseases, especially those that cause renal or hepatic insufficiency, may alter drug metabolism and hence can cause accumulation of drug in the body leading to toxicity.

Exogenous factors: The effect of one drug can be altered by simultaneous administration of another drug or even food. There can be synergistic, additive or antagonistic effects. Coadministration of NSAIDs with aspirin, alcohol, some antihypertensives, antidepressants, and other commonly used medications may cause drug interactions and adverse reactions. Sertraline interacts with alprazolam to cause neonatal respiratory distress syndrome. Prednisone causes decreased metabolism of cyclosporine leading to cyclosporine toxicity. Cranberry juicecan cause increase in INR.

Classification based on onset

Acute: Adverse effects which are seen within 60 minutes of drug administration.

Sub-acute: The time to onset of such reactions is 1 to 24 hours.

Latent: The resulting adverse effect is delayed, occurs after 2 days of administration of the drug.

Classification based on severity

Mild: Such adverse reactions are bothersome or tolerable. No change in therapy, antidote and prolongation of hospitalization is required.Example headache, nausea, vomiting, fatigue.

Moderate: Such reactions require change in therapy, treatment or hospitalization for atleast one day. Example allergic rashes, mood disorders

Severe: These are potentially life-threatening;they can cause permanent damage and can result to intensive medical treatment.Example renal failure, myocardial infraction, permanent deafness.

Lethal: Such reactionsdirectly or indirectly contribute to the death of the patient.Example cancer.

Classification based on cause

Type A (Augmented), Type B (Bizarre), Type C (Chronic), Type D (Delayed) , Type E (Exit/End of treatment), Type F (Lack of effect), Type G (Genotoxicity), Type H (Hypersensitivity), Type U (Unclassified)

Type A (Augmented): These are usually the extensions of normal pharmacological effect of a drug. They are common, dose-dependent, mild in nature, always predictable with known mechanism of action. Examples Bleeding caused by Warfarin and Anti-coagulants, Bronchospasm or Bradycardia associated with Beta-blockers, Deafness with Aminoglycosides.

Type B (Bizarre): Such reactions are idiocyncratic. The cause and mechanism is unknown.They are unpredictable, less common, not dose dependent. They are oftenly serious, as they may be discovered for the first time after a drug has been marketed. They can cause mortality. Example: Anaphylaxis in response to Penicillin.

Type C (Continuous/Chronic): They occur due to long term use of a drug often associated with dose accumulation. Such reactions are related to cumulative drug use. Example: Iatrogenic Cushing's syndrome with prednisolone.

Type D (Delayed): Suchreaction occurs due to prolonged use of a drugor exposure at a critical time which does not tend to accumulate. These are uncommon but dose dependent, includes carcinogenicity and mutagenicity. Examples: Leucopenia may be caused using Lomustine, Bladder Carcinoma after treatment with cyclophosphamide, Tardive dyskinesia caused by antipsychotic medication.

Type E (Exit/End of treatment): Such reactions occur when the patient has completed the treatment course, just after the drug is withdrawn. They include withdrawal effects of drug. Examples include rebound hypotension on clonidine discontinuation and opiate withdrawal syndrome.

Type F (Lack of effect): Failure of therapy is common, dose-related and often caused by drug interactions. The antibiotic resitance shown by micro-organisms comes under this category. There are various types of Lack of effect like:

Wearing off effect in which the disease symptoms reappear before the next dose remains due.

Drug effect incomplete in which the drug is able to cure some of the symptoms of the targeted disease but not all.

Drug effect variable in which the response of the drug to a particular indication is not fixed.

Delayed drug effect in which the drug starts to produce its effect after significant amout of time on administration.

Type G (Genotoxicity): Certain drugs may cause genetic alterations or damage. The teratogenic drugs produce chromosomal variations or genetic damage in fetus. Carcenogenic drugs can cause genetic variations.

Type H (Hypersensitivity): These are caused by allergen. They are most common reactions after type A. They usually involve antigen antibody reactions and hence associated with immunity. They are usually unpredictable and are not dose dependent.There are four types of hypersensitivity reactions:

- Type I : Anaphylactic reactions (Immediate type) in which the body responds to an antigen by producing a specific type of antibody, IgE. Example Anaphylaxis from β-lactam antibiotic. Antigens from fruits, grass/trees, fruits, animals, food or dairy products etc can produce such responses.
- Type II : Type 2 can also involve IgG and IgM antibodies. They can cause cytotoxic effects.Cytotoxic Example Hemolytic anemia from penicillin)
- Type III:These are mediated by IgG. Antigen- antibody complexes are formed in skin, blood vessels and hence lead to series of reactions causing tissue damage. They are also called Immune complex mediated reaction. Example: Serum sickness from anti-thymocyte globulin)
- Type IV: These are T-Cell mediated, delayed type. These reactions are further divided into type 4a, type 4b, type 4c, and type 4d based on the type of T cell involved and the reaction produced. Example Contact dermatitis from topical antihistamine.

Type U (Unclassified): There are some reactions whose mechanism of action is not understood and have not been categorised into any of the above classes.

Important Definitions

Intolerance: Drug intolerance or sensitivity is the inability to tolerate the adverse effects of a medication at therapeutic or subtherapeutic dose.Example, a few doses of Carbamazepine may cause ataxia in some children.

Drug Photosensitivity: A cutaneous reaction which occurs when the skin becomes highly sensitive to sunlight or UV radiation on application or administration of a drug. Such reactions are manifested in the form of skin rashes or sunburn with pain, blister or peel. Solar urticaria is the medical term for hives that appear after just a few minutes of exposure to sunshine.Photosensitivity is of two types: Phototoxic and photoallergic.

In phototoxic reaction, highly reactive oxygen molecules are formed that causes tissue damage. These are manifested as sunburn reactions. Such reactions have a quick onset after exposure within few minutes to hours. Photoallergic reactions are type IV hypersensitivity reactions resembling eczema. They usually develop within days (48-72 hours) and are less common than phototoxic reactions. Photoallergic reactions can also manifest in the areas that have not been exposed to the sun.

Drug dependence: Drug dependence is a state in which the drug is used for personal satisfaction mainly rather than basic therapeutic value, often in the face of known risks to health.

Psychological dependence is said to have developed when the individual is not capable of stopping drug usage and abuse drugs even when health problems arise.

Physical dependence is an altered physiological state produced by repeated administration of a drug which causes chemical level change in the brain due to their addictive nature. Discontinuation leads to withdrawal reactions.

Drug abuse refers to use of a drug by self-medication not for the therapeutic benefit but for the purposeof getting reward or feeling high (euphoria).

Drug addiction is a pattern of drug use characterized by overwhelming desire to take the drug and inability to stop it despite of the harmful consequences.

Drug habituation denotes less intensive involvement with the drug, so that its withdrawal produces only mild discomfort

Mutagenicity and Carcinogenicity: The ability of a drug to cause genetic mutation is known as mutagenicity whereas the ability to cause cancer is called as carcinogenicity. Oxidation of drug may lead to free radical formation which is higly reactive intermediate affecting the genetic makeup. Covalent interactions with DNA can also induce mutation. The modified DNA can code for various factors that causes cancer. Thus the drugs causing such side effects should not be used unless there is any life threatening condition.

Drug induced diseases: Certain drugs may cause diseases which persist even when the drug is withdrawn. These are called as iatrogenic agents. Example Hepatitis by isoniazid.

Serious adverse events

An adverse eventis serious and should be reported to FDA when it results in

- Death
- Life-threatening
- Initial hospitalization/Prolonged hospitalization
- Disability or permanent damage
- Conginetal anomaly/Birth defects
- Requires intervention to prevent damage
- Other serious or important medical events

CHAPTER TWO

Drug discovery and Clinical trial

As per Drug and Cosmetic act, drug includes all medications intended for internal or external use in humans or animals, as well as all compounds aimed at diagnosing, mitigating, treating, or preventing any disease or ailment in humans or animals, including preparations used topically to ward off insects like mosquitoes.

As may occasionally be specified by the Central Government by notification in the Official Gazette, such substances (other than food) intended to affect the structure or any function of the human body or meant to be used for the destruction of disease causing insects in human beings or animals.

Every ingredient intended to be used as a medication component, including bare gelatin capsules; and

After consulting with the Board, the Central Government may from time to time specify such devices by publication in the Official Gazette for internal or external use in the diagnosis, treatment, mitigation, or prevention of sickness or disorder in humans or animals.

Drug discovery and development is a process by which a drug comes into the market after passing various trials and experimentation. The process is not simple and it may take around 13-15 years for a drug to come in the market. The drug candidate has to go through various steps in the mean time. The procedure is quite time- and money-consuming.

Typically, screening for potentially active compounds is the first step in the early drug discovery process. Following their discovery, these substances are tested for safety and efficacy. They must have a therapeutic effect on the intended ailment. Only 1 out of every 5,000 medications typically reach the level of market approval. In addition, only 250 of the 5,000 to 10,000 therapeutic candidates advance to preclinical testing.

Objective of drug discovery

- To fulfill the unmet medical needs
- To get a cost-effective alternate medication
- To get a medicine with better therapeutic profile and minimal side effects compared to those already in the market
- To cure and palliate untreatable diseases
- To search for a medicine that can be manufactured easily.

Steps involved in drug discovery

The early drug discovery process includes target identification and validation.

Target identification: A drug target is a biological molecule, typically a protein, that is intrinsically linked to a specific disease process and that a drug could target to have the intended therapeutic effect. The requirements of the problematic ailment are typically taken into account when choosing a treatment target, therefore this stage is essentially biological or biochemical in nature. The target should ideally be linked to a disease and have an appropriate binding-pocket or active site where a medication or drug-like molecule can bind. In general, proteins make good targets, but RNA can occasionally be used in the same way. Enzymes are ideal therapeutic targets because they frequently include tiny grooves or nooks that a substrate (a small ligand) can easily attach to and block.

Target validation: Each prospective medication candidate is subject to a thorough screening process including 5000–10000 molecules. Scientists often validate a pharmacological target after they have confirmed interaction with it by comparing activity against the clinical condition for which the medicine is being produced.

High Throughput Screening:HTS involves automated screening of large number of compound against the biological target.

Lead identification: Lead compounds are substances that exhibit desired biological or pharmacological action and may serve as the starting point for the creation of a brand-new clinically relevant drug. Natural products, chemical libraries, and computational medicinal chemistry are potential sources of lead compounds and innovative medications.

Lead optimization: Next, lead candidates' structures are changed to better their properties. After being initially screened, lead compounds that are still viable are "optimised," or changed to make them more efficient and secure. Scientists can alter a compound's structure to change its qualities. For instance, they may reduce the likelihood of interaction with other chemical pathways in the body, hence lowering the possibility of adverse effects.

The **hit** is a molecule that interacts with the target to produce the desired therapeutic effect. High Content Screening, phenotypic screening, fragment-based screening, structure-based screening and virtual screening are some of the strategies used to discover hits.

Pre-clinical phase

With few optimized compounds, testing is done in non-humans. Preclinical studies, also known as non-clinical trials, are laboratory tests of a novel medicinal ingredient or medical technology, typically conducted on animal subjects to see whether the treatment actually works and whether testing on humans would be safe. The goal of pre-clinical studies is to determine the safety profile, the safe dose for human study, pharmacological activity and assess the toxicity of the investigational product. The experimentation on animals is controlled by Institutional Animal ethics committee (IAEC). Beside this experimentation on large animals are regulated by Committee for the Purpose of Control and Supervision of Experiments on Animals (CPCSEA). Animals commonly used for the study are mouse, rat, rabbit, guinea pig, and hamster. If the results on the small animals are successful, testing can be done in large animals like cat, dog, monkey.

There are various types of tests used in pre-clinical trials

- Screening test: Simple and rapid test to determine the pharmacodynamics profile.
- Tests on isolated organ or bacterial cell
- Tests on animal models like rat, mice, hamster
- Observational studies on mice in which drugs are given in 3 doses to observe the hidden effects.
- Confirmatory tests and other related activities: Compounds passing the preliminary tests are taken for more complex confirmatory tests.
- Tests to understand the Mechanism of action.
- Cardiovascular study: The first stage in identifying potential cardiovascular toxicity involves using assays to evaluate interactions with the hERG (human ether a go go) channels, which encode for the a-subunit of the Ikr channel, one of numerous cardiac channels involved in repolarization. The potential to lengthen the cardiac QT interval, a crucial criterion for which the ICH has given special guidelines, is thought to be indirectly assessed by the hERG channel interactions.
- Safety Pharmacology: As part of the safety pharmacology section of the IND application, regulatory bodies need a number of in vivo animal testing. These, as described in ICH Guideline S7A, are intended to identify unfavourable or hazardous NCE effects after acute delivery at therapeutic levels. According to

this recommendation, a core set of tests encompassing typical physiological assessments of heart, lung, and central nervous system health should be performed. An anaesthetized dog is used for the initial cardiovascular assessment, which also includes ECG and measures of blood pressure, heart rate, delayed ventricular depolarization, and other variables. While central nervous system effects are assessed by quantifying spontaneous motor activity, general behavioural activity, coordination, reflex reactions, and body temperature, respiratory assessment entails measuring respiratory rate, tidal volume, and oxygen saturation.

- Pharmacokinetic study: The dose-response relationship, ADME profile is tested.
- Toxicological profile: Two different species of animals are used in acute toxicity study. Drugs are administered through two different routes. The mortality is observed for one to three days to determine the lethal dose or the dose which kills 50% of the animals. Long term toxicity is studied using chronic and subchronic studies. Subchronic studies involves administration of the dose for 4 weeks to 3 months, chronic study is done for two years. For organ toxicity,histopathological studies are done. Some special toxicity studies like mutagenicity, teratogenicity and carcinogenicity are lso done. Local toxicity study involves local application of the drug candidate, example ocular toxicity, dermal toxicity and photosensitivity.

Good Laboratory Practices for animal research

The following guidelines should be followed:

a. An animal research facility should have a minimum of 6 to 12 rooms, each independently ventilated with 10 to 15 air exchanges, 450 lux illumination with 12-hour light/dark cycles, 60 decibel sound levels, and clean and service corridors to maintain the barrier.

b. Separate feed and bedding storage area with one room each.
c. There should be a washing area with a large autoclave facility.
d. There should be a separate necropsy area for postmortem.
e. DG established backup facilities for power outages.
f. Room for formulating and preparing reagents
g. There should be separate isolation area for the animals with diseases.
h. The cages, racks should be thoroughly cleaned at a regular interval of time.
a. Separate area for different species of animals
j. There should be appropriate refrigeration system.

IND

The researchers must submit an Investigational New Drug (IND) application to the FDA prior to starting any clinical trial.If the researcher want the approval in India only then same application can be submitted to DCGI. The preclinical research findings, the chemical make-up of the candidate medicine, how it is thought to function in the body, a list of any side effects, and manufacturing details are all included in the application. A thorough clinical trial design that describes how, where, and by whom the investigations will be carried out is also included in the IND. The FDA examines the application to ensure that clinical trial participants won't be exposed to unreasonably high risks. Additionally, IRB/IRC also reviews the safety and well-being of the participants at the site of clinical trial.

There are three types of IND:

Investigator IND: A doctor who both initiates and conducts a research and whose direct supervision the experimental drug is delivered or supplied must submit an Investigator IND. In order to examine an unapproved treatment, an approved product, or both for a new indication or in a new patient group, a doctor may file a research IND.

Emergency use IND: When an urgency arises and there isn't enough time to submit an IND in accordance with 21CFR, Sec. 312.23, or Sec. 312.20, the FDA may authorise the use of an investigational drug under the terms of an IND. It is also utilised for patients who don't fit the requirements of an established study protocol or when none is available.

Treatment IND: While the final clinical work is carried out and the FDA evaluation is taking place, an IND is submitted for investigational medications that have shown promise in clinical trials for serious or immediately life-threatening disorders.

The sponsor must wait 30 calendar days after submitting the IND before starting any clinical studies. The FDA has the chance to assess the IND during this time period for safety to ensure that research subjects won't be exposed to an excessive risk.

Clinical trials

Before the drug candidate can be launched into the market, it has to go through some extensive testing in human beings. Since the drugs are meant to be used in humans hence the test results obtained from animals cannot be relied on completely as the physiology of animals and humans are quite different. Hence the safety and efficacy of the drug candidate in humans should be established. By means of clinical trials, researchers may get answer of the questions, whether the treatment work, whether the drug has any side effect or whether it is better than other existing drugs.

Objective and need:

1) to test novel medications, medical equipment, biologics, or other treatments on people in carefully regulated scientific environments

2) necessary for innovative therapies to receive regulatory authority approval.

3) to evaluate the efficacy and safety of an investigational treatment

4) Determine whether the new intervention is superior to the current course of treatment.

5) to compare the effectiveness of two conventional or commercial therapies.

Clinical trial is conducted as per a plan called as protocol. The trial's schedule of tests, procedures, medications, and dosages, as well as the necessary follow-up and study duration, are all outlined in the plan. Additionally, it outlines the outcomes (endpoints) that will be assessed. Clinical trial is conducted in four different phases as per the GCP guidelines, each of these have different objectives or purposes.

There are usually four phases of clinical trials as described below

Phase I :

- Healthy human volunteers are selected with their informed consent.
- Around 20-80 participants are considered.
- Some drugs are very toxic like anticancer or antiHIV drugs and cause serious intolearable side effects in healthy people. Hence such drugs are directly administered to patients.
- Since healthy volunteers are mainly used in phase I trials hence we cannot check the efficacy of the drug as they do not have the particular diseaee or illness.
- The safety profile of the drug is analysed.
- The human equivalent dose calculated from the animal study is administered to the healthy volunteers.
- The participants are administered with single ascending dose or multiple ascending dose until the maximum tolerable dose is established (endpoint). Thus the safe and tolerable dose is established.
- These are performed in a single centre and takes around 3-6 months

Phase II:

- In this phase, patients are considered
- In early phase 20-200 patients are considered, they are administered with a single dose of drug
- The safety and efficacy of the drug candidate is checked. The detailed pharmacokinetic and pharmacodynamics data is analysed.
- Unicentric trial.
- In late phase, patients are administered with different doses of drug. (50-500 participants).
- The tests takes around 6 months to 2 years.

Phase III:

- These are pivotal studies
- Around 2000-5000 patients are considered from various areas (even can be selected from foreign countries as well) hence these are multicentric trial.
- The genetic profile of people varies according to their geographical location and hence the response of the drug candidate among various types of people can be determined.
- People of different age groups are considered.
- Thus phase III trials are used for confirming the safety and efficacy of the drug.
- All the participants do not receive the drug, some are provided with placebo and some receive standard drugs so that comparative study can be done.
- Blinding is another feature in which the receipient is unaware of the drug he/she has received (single-blinding) or both the patients as well as the physician are unaware about the drug being administered (double-blinding). Blinding is done to prevent the biasness involved in trial.

Phase IV:

- This trial is conducted after the drug has been approved by FDA for marketing.
- This is also known as post –marketing survellience
- This trial as no fixed duration. The number of subjects depend upon the trial endpoint
- They are conducted to identify the rare disease, long-term side effects, drug interactions, new indication of an existing drug.

Phase 0 (optional):

- Also known as micro-dosing study
- 10-15 healthy human volunteers are used.
- $1/100^{th}$ of the actual human dose is used
- Objective of this phase is to find out those possible drug candidates which reach the target.
- Some drug candidates do not reach the desired target or even they may accumulate in some other sites instead of accumulating at the desired site of action. Those drug candidates are not suitable and they are not considered for further study. Thus MAH are not required to investigate their time or money after the phase I/II/III trials.

NDA/ DOSSIER

A dossier is a group of documents pertaining to a specific subject. Any pharmaceutical preparation intended for human use must first go through the process of analysing and evaluating the pharmaceutical preparation's dossier, which includes comprehensive information on administrative, quality, non-clinical, and clinical data. This procedure, which is controlled and approved by a nation's drug regulatory agency, is known as the NDA in the USA, the MAA in the EU, and the Registration Dossier in other nations.

After the phase III trial is done, New Drug Application or NDA is submitted to FDA. FDA on the basis of NDA comes to the following key decision:

1) The drug's safety and efficacy for the intended usage, as well as if the advantages of the drug outweigh the disadvantages.

2) The appropriateness and content of the drug's proposed labelling (package insert).

3) Whether the processes utilised to make the medicine and the quality controls in place are sufficient to maintain the drug's identity, strength, quality, and purity.

A generic drug product's data is included in an abbreviated new drug application (ANDA), which is submitted to the FDA for assessment and possible approval. After receiving approval, an applicant is free to produce and market the generic drug product as a secure, affordable substitute for the brand-name medication it refers to.

CHAPTER THREE

Pharmaceutical Regulatory Authorities

Overview

A regulatory agency, sometimes known as a regulatory body, is a government entity that has the jurisdiction to issue licences and regulate certain types of human activity. These are typically put in place to increase safety and standards and/or to shield the general public and the federal government from unethical corporate practises in markets where there is a dearth of healthy competition or a risk of an excessive exercise of monopoly power.

Health Authorities are the governmental bodies in charge of enforcing health laws worldwide. They perform crucial governmental functions for safeguarding and ensuring the public's health.

USFDA

One of the federal executive departments of the United States is the Department of Health and Human Services, which includes the US Food and Drug Administration (FDA). In 1906, it was founded. The FDA is in charge of regulating and overseeing the safety of food, tobacco products, dietary supplements, prescription and over-the-counter medications, vaccines, biopharmaceuticals, blood transfusions, medical devices, electromagnetic radiation emitting devices (ERED), and veterinary products in order to protect and promote public health. It has nine locations or offices and is headquartered in Maryland, USA.

Forms from Medwatch are utilised for FDA Safety Reporting. The MedWatch system gathers reports of unfavourable responses and poor quality (E.g.; All type of clinical and spontaneous reports and special scenarios like lack of effect, pregnancy, medication error).

While Form 3500A is a mandated reporting form used by IND reports, makers, distributors, importers, and user facility staff, Form 3500B is for use by healthcare professionals, consumers, and patients.

Report issues with e-cigarettes (often referred to as "vapes"), e-liquids, heated tobacco products, cigarettes, roll-your-own cigarettes, cigars, small cigars, pipes, waterpipes (commonly referred to as hookah), chewing tobacco, and snuff. Contact the Safety Reporting Portal with any problems. Involve the Vaccine Adverse Event Reporting System (VAERS) in vaccine-related incidents. Report a Problem to the Center for Veterinary Medicine to report issues with animal medications, equipment, or meals, including pet foods.

CDER (Centre for Drug Evaluation and Research): By ensuring that safe and effective medications are available to improve people's health in the United States, the Center for Drug Evaluation and Research (CDER) fulfils a crucial public health function. CDER, a division of the U.S. Food and Drug Administration (FDA), oversees the regulation of both prescription and OTC medications, including biological therapies and generic medications. There is more to our work than just medications. Drugs include things like sunscreen, fluoride toothpaste, antiperspirants, and dandruff shampoos.

CBER (Center for Biologics Evaluation and Research): CBER is the division under FDA that regulates biological products for human use. It does so in compliance with pertinent federal laws, such as the Public Health Service Act and the Federal Food, Drug and Cosmetic Act.By ensuring that biological products are secure, efficient, and available to people who require them, CBER promotes and protects public health. Additionally, CBER disseminates knowledge to the general public to encourage the responsible and safe use of biological products.

CDRH (Center for Devices and Radiological Health): The CDRH is in charge of safeguarding and advancing public health. The organisation makes sure that safe, effective, and high-quality medical devices and safe radiation-emitting items are available to patients and healthcare professionals in a timely manner. They provide easily intelligible and accessible science-based information on the items we regulate to consumers, patients, their carers, and physicians. By improving regulatory science, offering the industry predictable, consistent, transparent, and effective regulatory processes, and ensuring consumer confidence in devices marketed in the U.S., they facilitate the creation of medical devices.

EMA

- European Agency for Evaluation of Medicinal Products, a decentralised organisation, existed throughout Europe from 1995 until 2004. It changed its name to EMA in 2004.
- The objectives are to offer objective, scientific advice on the effectiveness, safety, and quality of medications as well as on broader topics pertaining to public and animal health that involve medications. Applications for European marketing authorization of pharmaceuticals are evaluated scientifically. The pharmaceutical industry is encouraged to innovate and do

research.

- Launched in December 2001, the European EudraVigilance system (the reporting system in the EU) deals with the electronic exchange of ICSRs, early detection of potential safety signals from commercially available drugs, monitoring and evaluating potential safety issues, and ongoing monitoring and evaluating potential safety issues.
- EVCTM: The EudraVigilance Clinical Trial Module facilitate the electronic reporting of Suspected Unexpected Serious Adverse Reaction(SUSARs).
- EVPM: The EudraVigilance Post – Authorization Module is designed for post-authorization ICSRs.

MHRA

The United Kingdom's government agency is called the Medicines and Healthcare Products Regulatory Agency (MHRA) (in Europe). It was established on April 1, 2003, when the Medical Devices Agency and the Medicines Control Agency (MCA) merged (MDA).The agency is responsible for:

- Ensuring that drugs, medical equipment, and blood components for transfusion adhere to appropriate safety, effectiveness, and quality criteria
- Ensuring the secure and safe flow of drugs, medical supplies, and blood components
- Supporting global harmonisation and standardisation to guarantee the efficacy and safety of biological therapies
- Contributing to the public's and healthcare professionals' knowledge of the advantages and disadvantages of medications, medical equipment, and blood components to promote their safer and more efficient usage.

- Promoting public health-related innovation and research and development
- Having an impact on regulatory frameworks at the UK, EU, and worldwide levels to ensure that they are risk-appropriate and successful at preserving public health.

MHLW

Ministry of Health, Labour and Welfare

- One of the cabinet-level ministries that establishes guidelines for maximum residual limits for agricultural chemicals in foods, fundamental rules for food and drugs, food additive standards, etc.
- Its headquarters are in Japan.
- Pharmaceutical and Medical Device Agency (PMDA) has jurisdiction over drug rules, while MHLW has the final say.
- Danger alerts and other medication safety information are sent by the Institute for Safe Pharmaceutical Practices (ISMP), a national system for reporting medication errors in a discreet manner.

PvPI

- The National Pharmacovigilance Program (NPVP) was launched in New Delhi on November 23, 2004. At the Central Drug Standard Control Organization (CDSCO) office, the programme is coordinated.

- In collaboration with the Department of Pharmacology at the All India Institute of Medical Sciences (AIIMS), New Delhi, the Central Drugs Standard Control Organization (CDSCO),

Directorate General of Health Services, under the auspices of the Ministry of Health & Family Welfare, Government of India, has launched a national pharmacovigilance programme to safeguard patients' health by ensuring the safety of their medications. As a National Coordinating Center, the Department of Pharmacology at AIIMS oversees the initiative (NCC). A Steering Committee will be in charge of managing the center's operations.

- In addition to informing healthcare professionals and the public about hazards, the Pharmacovigilance Programme of India (PvPI), which is coordinated by the National Coordination Centre of the Indian Pharmacopoeia Commission in Ghaziabad, collects data, analyses it, and draws conclusions.
- The intention is to protect Indian public health by ensuring that the advantages of using medicine exceed the risks.

ICH

An innovative project called the International Conference on Harmonization of Technical Requirements for Registration of Pharmaceuticals for Human Use brings together regulatory agencies from Europe, Japan, and the USA with professionals from the pharmaceutical industry in each of the three countries to discuss the scientific and technical facets of product registration. It was established on April 1st, 1990.

In order to discuss and produce ICH recommendations, the International Council for Harmonization of Technical Requirements for Pharmaceuticals for Human Use (ICH) brings together regulatory agencies and the pharmaceutical sector. Since its founding in 1990, ICH has gradually changed to adapt to more worldwide trends in the pharmaceutical industry, and an increasing number of regulatory authorities are using these ICH standards. In order to ensure that safe, effective, and high-quality medications are produced, registered, and maintained in the most resource-efficient manner while fulfilling high standards, ICH's aim is to achieve greater global harmonisation. ICH has expanded as an organisation and now has 20 Members and 35 Observers since announcing organisational modifications in October 2015.

Four categories (QSEM)

Quality: Chemical and pharmaceutical Quality Assurance (Stability Testing, Impurity Testing, etc.)

Safety: In vitro and in vivo pre-clinical studies (Carcinogenicity Testing, Genotoxicity Testing, etc.)

Efficacy: Clinical studies in human subject (Dose Response Studies, Good Clinical Practices, etc.)

Multidisciplinary: Cross-cutting

Goals

- Making suggestions to achieve better uniformity in the interpretation and application of technical standards and guidelines for the registration of pharmaceutical products and the maintenance of such registrations;
- Maintaining a venue for a fruitful discussion of scientific matters between regulatory agencies and the pharmaceutical industry regarding the harmonisation of technical requirements for pharmaceutical products;
- Contributing to the protection of public health in the interest of patients from a global perspective;
- Monitoring and updating harmonised technical requirements leading to a greater mutual acceptance of research and development data;
- Avoiding divergent outcomes
- To make it simpler for new or improved technical research and development methods to replace or upgrade existing processes;
- To promote the proper use and integration of common standards through the coordination of training on standardised guidelines and their use as well as their dissemination, communication, and information sharing;

- Create policies for the ICH Medical Dictionary for Regulatory Activities Terminology (MedDRA), while ensuring its technical and scientific upkeep, development, and dissemination as a standardised dictionary that facilitates the exchange of regulatory data for human-use pharmaceuticals across international borders.

Efficacy guidelines

○ E2A : Expedited Clinical Safety Reporting
○ E2B(R3) :Data elements to be transferred in ICSR.
○ E2C(R2) : Periodic benefit-risk evaluation report (PBRER)
○ E2D : Postmarketing expedited Reporting Standards
○ E2E : Pharmacovigilance Planning
○ E2F : Development Safety Update Report

WHO-UMC

○ WHO set up a programme in 1978 which is carried out by Upsala Monitoring Centre in Sweden.
○ VIGIBASE database for ICSR linked to WHO-ART, MedDRA, WHO-ICD , WHO DD.
○ Features include coordinating the WHO's global drug monitoring programme, gathering, evaluating, and disseminating data from member nations on the advantages, dangers, and effectiveness of medications, working together with member nations to develop and implement pharmacovigilance, bringing promising drugs to the attention of regulatory authorities in member nations.

CIOMS

WHO and UNESCO together founded the Council for International Organizations of Medical Sciences (CIOMS), an international, non-governmental, non-profit organisation, in 1949. Through its member organisations, which include many of the biomedical disciplines, national academies of sciences, and medical research councils, CIOMS represents a sizeable percentage of the biomedical scientific community. Through advice on health research and policy, including ethics, medical product development, and safety, CIOMS aims to enhance public health. CIOMS is an associate partner of UNESCO and has official links with WHO.

Country	Regulatory Agency
USA	Food and Drug Administration (FDA)
Europe	European Medicines Agency (EMEA)
Japan	The Pharmaceuticals and Medical Devices Agency (PMDA)
Australia	Therapeutic Goods Administration (TGA)
China	State Food and Drug Administration(SFDA)

CHAPTER FOUR

Aggregate Reporting

The periodical news of combination safety reports to regulatory health authorities includes a comprehensive outline of the protection profile of healthful product supported accumulative safety information accumulated by promoting Authorization Holder (MAH). They put together supply assurance that the MAH is endlessly observation and critically assessing the benefit-risk profile of the merchandise and taking applicable risk minimizing actions where new safety concerns or changes to existing problems with safety ar glorious. The international commonplace for periodic reports follows news pointers set by the International Conference on Harmonization (ICH).

In addition to submission of Individual case safety reports (ICSRs), MAH is obligated to report the accumulative safety exposure information in periodical intervals to many health authorities at intervals the required timelines that in turn depends on age of healthful product inside the market and type of combination report. This continued observation on combination safety information facilitates regulators and MAH to stay up positive profit risk balance and implementing the primary risk diminution plans for safety concerns reportable.

Combination Safety Reports serve the following purposes:

1. To assess and update global safety knowledge with a healthy product at specified time points, before and after approval

2. to provide a brief summary of safety information together with a study of the product's profit risk profile.

3. To determine whether the security data requires further research or revisions to the label of an authorised healthy product.

4. In accordance with the general pointers

Types of Aggregate reports

Different types of reports, such as pre-approval aggregate safety reports and post-approval aggregate safety reports, are generated by MAH according on the stage of the marketing authorisation.

Aggregate reports for pre-approval: It contains a comprehensive review of the safety data for compounds still undergoing clinical testing. It often comprises data on subject safety from clinical trial participants as well as safety information from non-clinical investigations.

Annual safety reports (ASRs) in Europe and IND annual reports

The number of reports produced was reduced as a result of the replacement of these two documents with the development safety update report (DSUR), which is a well-aligned document that allows health regulators in the three ICH areas to get the same information simultaneously.

2. Post-approval mixture reports: they supply the additive outline of safety info for the healthful merchandise from the selling exposure. The sources of safety information embrace Non-clinical, clinical studies and Non international studies, literature articles and spontaneous cases.

The following styles of reports ar submitted for healthful merchandise post selling authorisation.

- PADER (Periodic adverse drug expertise report)
- Periodic profit Risk analysis Report (PBRER)/ Periodic safety update report (PSUR)
- supplement to clinical overviews (ACO)
- Risk management arrange (RMP)

Timelines and restrictive requirements:

DSUR: the event safety update report (DSUR) is pre-marketing periodic report that covers safety info of medication, biological, vaccines and jazz group merchandise beneath development (including marketed medication that ar beneath any study) among the ICH regions.

DSUR for single active moiety and combined products:

A single DSUR as well as safety information from all clinical trials conducted with the drug ought to

be ready for associate investigational drug:

1. All indications

2. All dose forms

3. All meant populations

For combined products: one DSUR ought to be ready for clinical trials involving a hard and fast combination product (.e., a product consisting of a minimum of 2 active ingredients during a fastened dose that's administered during a single dose form). If the sponsor is additionally conducting clinical trials with individual component(s) of the fastened combination product, separate DSUR(s) ought to be submitted for every element.

Objective:

The main objective of a DSUR is to gift a comprehensive, thoughtful annual review and analysis of pertinent safety info collected throughout the reportage amount associated with a drug beneath investigation, whether or not or not it's marketed, by:

• Examining whether or not information|the data} obtained by the sponsor throughout the reportage amount is in unison with previous knowledge of the investigational drug's safety

• Describing new questions of safety that would have an impression on the protection of run subjects

• summarizing the present understanding and management of known and potential risks

• providing associate update on the standing of the clinical investigation/development program and study results.

The DSUR includes safety info of active moiety from:

1. All in progress clinical trials and different studies that the sponsor is conducting or has completed throughout the review amount

2. Empiric or medicine studies

3. Nonclinical studies (toxicological and in vitro studies)

4. connected DSURs, if applicable to the investigational drug

5. producing or microbiological changes

6. Studies recently printed within the literature

7. Clinical trials with results indicating lack of effectualness that would have a right away impact

When to submit DSUR:

There is one, harmonious biological process International Birthdate (DIBD) that is that the 1st authorization from a administrative body to the sponsor to try to to a run anyplace within the world. this may need the restrictive cluster within the company to convey this info to any or all of the concerned health agencies in order that the birthdate is harmonious. Since there's a famed fastened schedule for submission, there'll be a hard and fast, single information lockpoint sixty days before submission for every DSUR.

In most countries the DSUR is submitted annually. corporations that have open INDs and NDAs (or the ex-US equivalents like CTCs/CTXs and MAs respectively) may additionally have their restrictive departments harmonize the birthdate for DSURs and PSURs such there's one submission date.

Recipients of DSUR

• restrictive Authorities: DSUR; inside sixty days from the DIBD

• EC/IRB, if required: government outline (plus line listing of SADRs)

• Final DSUR during a Territory: are notified with a canopy letter.

PBRER/PSUR: The Benefit-risk analysis ought to be distributed throughout the lifecycle of the healthful product to push and shield public health and to reinforce patient safety through effective risk step-down plans and implementations. once a selling authorization is granted, it's necessary to continue evaluating the advantages and risks of healthful merchandise in actual use and/or long run use, to verify that the benefit-risk profile remains favourable.

The date once sponsor received authorisation for selling a drug is taken into account as International birth date (IBD) of the healthful product. information lock purpose is that the point in time for completion of reportage interval. PBRER could be a advanced report with twenty sections as well as appendices compared to DSUR and PADER. The timeline for these post approval mixture reports varies supported the age of healthful product within the market including the subsequent varieties of reportage intervals and their various restrictive timelines.

Reporting interval category	Criteria for medicinal products	Regulatory timeline
6 month reporting interval	Newly approved and marketed for 1 year period	70 calendar days
Annual reporting interval	In market for more than 1 year	90 calendar days
Multilayer reporting Interval	In market for more than 5 years	90 calendar days

How to Prepare a PBRER:

A Single PBRER for an Active Drug: The report must include a single DLP and detail all approved dosages, regimens, and indications for the active substance.

PBRER for Fixed-Dose Combination Product: Depending on the circumstances, information for fixed combinations of drugs that are also sold separately may be reported in a separate PBRER/PSUR or included as distinct presentations in the report for one of the component substances.

Products Produced and/or marketed by Multiple Companies: Each MAH is in charge of filing PSURs for its own goods.

When businesses are involved in contractual arrangements (such as licensor-licensee relationships), the written agreement should explicitly state each party's responsibility for preparing and submitting the PSUR to the regulatory authorities.

Here is a quick explanation of the main author's duties throughout PBRER preparation.

• A timetable for kick-off meetings with several stakeholders who will provide information to various report parts. (Teams in signal management, finance/sales, clinical, and medical regulation)

• Talking about the action items and their associated deadlines

• Obtaining and reconciling line listings (ICSR cases from safety database)

• Creation of a draught PBRER report using the safety data gathered from various stakeholders.

• Internal quality and medical review • Modifications to the draught report as needed in response to reviewer comments

• Final report approval • Submission of PBRER to the appropriate regulatory body (70th or 90th calendar day)

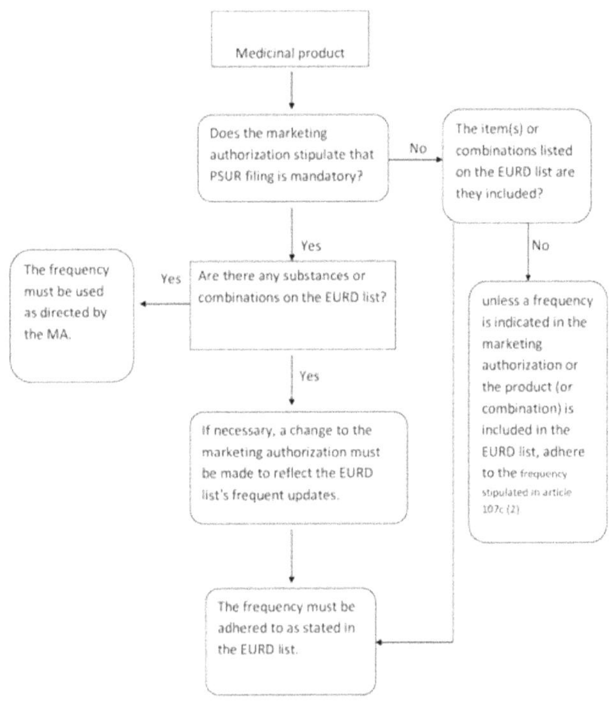

Concept of submission of PSURs

PADER: A post-marketing safety report known as the Periodic Adverse Drug Experience Report is delivered to the US Food and Drug Administration (USFDA). The major goal is to present summary statistics with an evaluation of the benefit risk profile of an authorised medicinal product from the post marketing exposure. The focus of PADER is on serious, unlisted instances with succinct narratives and summaries of ICSR reports over the previous 15 days. It also covers the safety-related regulatory actions that were taken throughout the reporting period since the last PADER was reported.

Reporting Interval category	Criteria for medicinal products	Regulatory timeline
Quarterly	For First three years, after marketing authorization	30 calendar days
Annual	In market for more than 2 years	60 calendar days

Table of Contents for a PADER:

• A narrative outline ANd analysis of the data within the report and an analysis of the 15-day alert reports submitted throughout the news interval (all 15-day alert reports should befittingly reference the applicant's patient positive identification, adverse reaction term(s), and date of submission to the FDA).

• A MedWatch kind (3500A) for every adverse drug expertise not reportable as a fifteen day accelerated report (with AN index consisting of a line listing of the applicant's patient positive identification and adverse reaction term(s)).

• A history of actions taken since the last report due to adverse drug experiences (e.g., labeling changes or studies initiated).

• Periodic news, aside from data concerning 15-day alert reports, does not

Apply to adverse drug expertise data obtained from postmarketing studies (whether or not they were conducted underneath AN investigational New Drug Application), from reports within the scientific literature, or from foreign selling expertise.

• Follow-up data to adverse drug experiences submitted in a very periodic report could also be submitted within the next periodic report.

As regulated by the federal agency, organizations have to be compelled to submit these reports once in a very quarter for 3 years inside thirty days of shut of quarter and later ought to submit these reports annually inside sixty days people approval date. The PADER / PAER submissions square measure only to be created in utterly electronic format, i.e. in electronic Common Technical Document (CTD).

CHAPTER FIVE

Signal detection and management

Introduction

Every pharmaceutical medication that has been approved for use in a controlled context has established advantages but is also associated with side effects. The prompt discovery of such unknown dangers is critical to the patient's safety. The detection approach is applicable to all pharmaceutical products and covers their full life cycle, including clinical development and post-market phases, for any form of adverse event, significant or minor. In pharmacovigilance, signal detection and management entails continuing monitoring of individual case safety reports (ICSR) to identify case reports or case report series of adverse events (AE) that need further inquiry and may necessitate safety actions such as a safety signal investigation. Signals are traditionally detected either subjectively or quantitatively. The former entails qualitative analysis via manual evaluation of individual case safety reports (ICSR) on an individual or cumulative basis. The latter, on the other hand, incorporates the more prevalent quantitative method that employs statistical tools, the most popular of which is disproportionality analysis.

Data mining is the most commonly utilised tool for identifying disproportionate reporting ratios. Data mining techniques, also known as signal disproportionality analysis (SDAs), are used to analyse a wide range of spontaneous report databases. This analysis aids in the discovery of previously undiscovered connections between pharmaceutical goods and reported adverse events (AEs) that may have slipped detection during the manual case evaluation. Quantitative signal detection, or more particularly disproportionality analysis, is accomplished by comparing the percentage of spontaneous ICSRs to the proportion that would be predicted if no relationship between the medical product and the event occurred. There are several methods for calculating disproportionality. The most prevalent methods are as follows:

The proportional reporting ratio (PRR) or the reporting odds ratio (ROR), as well as Bayesian approaches such as the multi-item gamma Poisson shrinker (MGPS) and the information component, are examples of such measures (IC). To detect adverse medication responses, a comprehensive study of spontaneous reports is undertaken (ADRs). Operators' SDAs and the nature of their reporting databases differ. Given the variety of contexts, it is questionable if any method can be anticipated to predict or estimate an ADR reliably. Although the present clinical assessment depends heavily on disproportionality analysis, it is entirely based on aggregate numbers of reports and so ignores the quality and type of the report's content.

As previously stated, the signal management process consists of the following steps:
1) Detection of signals
2) Signal verification
3) Prioritization of signals
4) Signal evaluation,
5) Action recommendation, and
6) Information exchange

Traditional software solutions frequently lack a viable user interface for total signal control. The explosion of solicited and unsolicited safety reports has resulted in an exponential increase in data volume over the previous decade. This will lead to more and more changes in surveillance data, which will be published in the following years. However, not only is the number of safety cases growing, but so are the sources and types of records, such as reports from electronic health records and claims, personal health records, health data standards, data from Federal and private sector mobile devices for tracking health, and data from social websites (blogs, patient advocacy group sites, and search term logs). To address such issues, a sophisticated signal management system would be necessary.

VigiRank

A data-driven screening method for finding possible, causally related safety warnings can be an effective hybrid technique. It takes into account report quality and substance, as well as disproportionate reporting. The predictive vigiRank method is used on the generated vigiRank variables to recognise and prioritise signals. Disproportionality reporting ratio (particularly IC), recent reporting, geographic dispersion, informative reports, time-to-onset, dechallenge, rechallenge, alone reported, and numerous reporting elements are the computed variables. The approach was developed using LASSO logistic regression using data from the FDA Adverse Event Reporting System (FAERS) dataset.

After recognising safety signals on the fly, the next step is signal prioritising. vigiRank generates a score as an output. This score might be used as an extra consideration in this step. Prioritizing signals with critical medical issues can be accomplished by using reaction outcomes or the seriousness attributes. The European Medicines Agency (EMA) has established a list of severe incidents known as designated medical events (DMEs). This list serves as a significant complicating element in signal prioritising. The EMA proposes that signals associated with these occurrences be given high priority regardless of the disproportionality ratios, and that one should not rely only on this list.

Important medical event (IME) is another type of list that aids in prioritising. Similarly, each pharmaceutical business will have its own list of targeted medical events (TMEs) for its drugs.

Signal validation entails verifying a signal analytically as well as via existing literature. The literature may be obtained in the form of research publications on sites such as PubMed, drug-labelling information sites, and so on. Analytical charts provide clarity on data such as gender distribution, proportion of reports with certain drug characteristics, and so on. This phase functions as an initial evaluation for each detected signal. Following validation, each signal may be classified into one of three categories: (1) legitimate signal, (2) not a signal, and (3) worthy of further investigation.

The following are the numerous aspects that are relevant in this phase, according to the EMA GVP Module IX:
• Prior knowledge of the response, as well as accessible data on the summary of product characteristics (SmPC) of pharmaceutical goods
• Evidence strength, such as disproportionality, data quality, dose-response relationship, and so on.
• Clinical relevance and context, such as a knowledge of drug-drug interactions, severity, and medication mistakes.

Thus, the solution given includes, but is not limited to, PubMed and medication label literature review, summary functionality, annotations, and graphs to display various statistical numbers. To control the flow of a signal, sections such as 'Open Signals,' 'Closed Signals,' 'Further Evaluation,' 'Keep Under Monitoring,' and 'Archive' are constructed, and all of these parts include tables reflecting all of the signals present at that stage of signal management.

Datasets

Volumes of medical data were thoroughly studied when developing the solution to demonstrate the scalability, resilience, and excellence of the suggested system.

The findings are summarised here, with the following caveats:

a) FAERS is the FDA's public spontaneous adverse event reporting system. Its data is accessible.

b) EudraVigilance is an open safety database maintained by the EMA.

c) In the signal validation step, each medicinal product's drug-labelling information is utilised.

d) The Cochrane Library and PubMed are examined to validate current research literature and reviews for a specific drug-event combination.

Signal detection and management

A noxious and intended reaction to a medicine that occurs at levels commonly employed in people for disease prevention, diagnosis, or therapy, or for the change of physiological function. An active surveillance system collects case safety information in a systematic and ongoing manner. The system does spontaneous reporting, in which case reports of adverse occurrences are willingly provided. Health practitioners and pharmaceutical producers submit these cases to national regulatory monitoring bodies. A signal is information that has been disclosed about a probable causal association between an adverse event and a medicine that was previously unknown or incompletely documented.

An unpleasant incident is divided into four categories:

1) Severity: Mild, moderate, or severe

2) Seriousness: Non-serious or serious

3) Expectedness: Expected or unexpected

4) Causality: Related or unrelated

ADRs are caused by a variety of causes, including:

• a lack of pharmacology understanding, adverse medication effects, and irrational drug usage, as well as improper prescription habits.
• Promotional efforts by pharmaceutical business detailers
• Lack of credible information sources
• Liberal drug outlets and harmful pharmaceutical practises
• Liberal over-the-counter (OTC) and self-medication methods

A signal is a potential link between AE and medications. The link between the adverse occurrence and a medicine was previously unknown or incompletely described. A signal is usually generated by more than one report. A signal is believed to be examined further based on its properties such as severity, event reaction consequence, and information quality. It cannot be considered definitive because the signal must be evaluated and validated. To produce a signal, traditional ways employ data mining algorithms. There are several database-related difficulties that must be addressed.

The following are solutions to challenges associated with data mining for databases:
• Incomplete, erroneous, or ambiguous information
• Multiple reports on the same occurrence
• Events might be caused by the treated condition, another condition, or a different product
• Over-reporting
• Reporting and processing timeliness

Conclusion

We examined signal recognition, signal prioritisation, signal validation, how a signal is handled in native techniques, its weaknesses, and how to solve such issues utilising hybrid methodology in this study. Though signal identification is our main goal, signal management is also an important problem we must address. We also talked about the prediction algorithm-based tools vigiRank and vigiGrade, which may assist anticipate a score as an output for each signal. In Part 2, we also developed hybrid approaches that include significant signal management strategies to create unambiguous results for users while dealing with the ever-increasing size of the report database without compromising the timeliness of identifying possible safety hazards and prioritising them.

CHAPTER SIX

Causality Assessment

Overview

Causality assessment is one of the most important as well as challenging part of pharmacovigilance.

Today the market is flooded with different drugs which cause different side effects apart from the beneficial effects. A patient can consume many of the drugs concomitantly. As a result it is quite common to have drug interactions or adverse drug reactions. The patient may also suffer from various comorbidities which also has influence in causing the untoward reactions. So it is not easy to blame each of the drugs for causing an adverse event. Hence the identification of the culprit drug from the mass is important as it can be life saving or helpful in preventing the further damage caused by the drug to our body systems. The safety of a patient is more important than the efficacy of the drugs and hence in the pursuit of the efficacy, safety should not be ignored. So the causality assessment tool helps to identify the particular culprit drug responsible for causing the untoward effect. In other words it is an evaluation of the likelihood that a particular treatment is the cause of an observed adverse event. So it can be identified whether a particular adverse event is adverse drug reaction or not. It is an essential part of adverse drug reactions report and important task conducted by National Pharmacovigilance Programme in each country. There are multiple criteria or algorithms available as of now for establishing a causal relationship in cases of adverse drug reaction (ADR) but none of them is specific or complete.

Objective

- Provide relationship between drug and events
- Signal detection
- Better evaluation of benefit-risk profile
- Evaluation of ADR in early warning system and regulatory reporting purposes.
- Aid in writing PBRER [2]

Method of assessment

In general, there exists no universally accepted method for accessing causality. Some of the existing methods were developed based upon temporal relationship, pharmacological plausibility, existing information about the ADR, absence of any competitive factors (like other drugs, diseases), dechallenge, rechallenge and drug interactions.

1. Expert judgement or Global introspection which includes Swedish methods and WHO-UMC causality assessment criteria.
2. Algorithms like Naranjo scale, Kramer algorithm, Jones algorithm, Adverse Drug Reactions Advisory Committee guidelines.

3. Probabilistic methods like Bayesian Methods, Australian method.

Bradford Hill's criteria

Hill's criteria for causation, also known as the Bradford Hill criteria, are a set of nine guidelines that might be helpful in generating epidemiologic proof of a causal connection between a suspected source and an observed effect.

Strength: A strong association between the cause and effect means more causal; small association does not mean that there is no causal relationship.

Consistency: The results produced should be consistent or reroducible in different places.

Specificity: The more specific the association between a factor and result is, the more it is causal.

Temporality: The effect is only possible after the cause.

Biological gradient: The greater is the exposure to a dose, the greater would be the response or effect. But in some cases, an inverse proportion is also observed.

Plausability: A reliable mechanism between cause and effect is necessary.

Coherence:A coherent relationship between epidemiological and laboratory findings increases the likelihood of an effect.

Experimental evidence: If the association between the cause and effect is proved experimentally, the greater would be the causation.

Analogous evidence: If a condition analogus to the cause causes a condition analogus to the effect then it can be depicted that the cause leads to the effect.

Expert judgement

This method is completely based upon the experience and knowledge about the subject matter. The WHO-UMC criteria is one of the popular method.

In WHO-UMC method, the assessement is based upon the following criteria:

1. Time interval between start of the drug and the onset of the adverse event.
2. Absence of any competitive factors like interacting drugs, disease states or comorbidities.
3. Dechallenge
4. Rechallenge

Dechallengeis the process of withdrawing a drug usually after an adverse event or after a planned treatment and recording the outcome of the event. If the outcome is recovered then it is positive dechallenge and if it does not disappear then the dechallenge is negative.

Rechallengerefers to the process of restarting of the same drug it has been stopped for an adverse event.If the adverse effect for which the drug was stopped recur, the rechallenge is said to be positive. For positive dechallenge to occur, AE had to have previously disappeared after the dechallenge. Negative dechallenge is the case where the adverse event does not recur after the drug is restarted.

Prechallenge: This is a newish term that refers to the use of the same drug at some point in the past.

There are six level of causality association in WHO-UMC method.

- CERTAIN
- PROBABLE/LIKELY
- POSSIBLE
- UNLIKELY
- CONDITIONAL/UNCLASSIFIED

- UNASSESSABLE/UNCLASSIFIABLE

Certain means interval between the start of the drug and the onset of the event is reliable and the patient neither has a concomitant disease norhas taken any competiting drugs.The dechallenge and rechallenge has to be positive.

Probable: For probable, there is no need of rechallenging. .The interval between the start of the drug and the onset of the event should be reasonable. Dechallenge has to be positive.

Possible: For possible there might exists some other factors associated with causing adverse event apart from the suspected drug. There is no dechallenge or rechallenge.

Unlikely: The time relationship between drug start and event onset is totally unreliable and presence of other factors to cause adverse event is more likely.

Unclassified/Conditional: The term unclassified is used when the existing data is insufficient and hence more information is required, such information is already under investigation.

Unassessable/Unclassifiable: When the existing information is incomplete or contradictory and it is not possible to collect more information, then unassessable is used.

Causality term	Assessment criteria
Certain	Event or laboratory test abnormality, with plausible time relationship to drug intake
	Cannot be explained by disease or other drugs
	Response to withdrawal Plausible (pharmacologically, pathologically)
	Event definitive pharmacologically or phenomenologically (i.e., an objective and specific medical disorder or a recognised pharmacological phenomenon)
	Rechallenge satisfactory, if necessary
Probable or likely	Event or laboratory test abnormality, with reasonable time relationship to drug intake
	Unlikely to be attributed to disease or other drugs
	Response to withdrawal clinically reasonable
	Rechallenge not required
Possible	Event or laboratory test abnormality, with reasonable time relationship to drug intake
	Could also be explained by disease or other drugs
	Information on drug withdrawal may be lacking or unclear
Unlikely	Event or laboratory test abnormality, with a time to drug intake that makes a relationship improbable (but not impossible)
	Disease or other drugs provide plausible explanations
Conditional or unclassified	Event or laboratory test abnormality
	More data for proper assessment needed, or additional data under examination
Unassessable/ unclassifiable	Report suggesting an adverse reaction
	Cannot be judged because information is insufficient or contradictory
	Data cannot be supplemented or verified

Naranjo method

The Adverse Drug Reaction (ADR) Probability Scale, often known as the Naranjo Scale, was created in 1991 by Naranjo and colleagues at the University of Toronto.This is a widely accepted method designed for use in controlled trials and registration studies of new medications, rather than in routine clinical practice. This method consists of ten questions that are answered as yes, know or unknown. Based upon the scores obtained, the classifications definite, probable, possible and doubtful are used.

Total Score ≥9	**Definite**. The reaction (1) followed a reasonable temporal sequence after a drug or in which a toxic drug level had been established in body fluids or tissues, (2) came after a known reaction to the suspected drug, (3) was validated by improvement after drug withdrawal, and returned after reexposure.
Total Score 5 to 8	**Probable**. The reaction (1) followed a reasonable temporal sequence after a drug, (2) followed a recognized response to the suspected drug, (3) was confirmed by withdrawal but not by exposure to the drug, and (4) could not be reasonably explained by the known characteristics of the patient's clinical state.
Total Score 1 to 4	**Possible**. The reaction (1) followed a temporal sequence after a drug, (2) possibly followed a recognized pattern to the suspected drug, and (3) could be explained by characteristics of the patient's disease.
Total Score ≤0	**Doubtful**. The reaction was likely related to factors other than a drug.

Kramer causality assessment scale

This algorithm is used to evaluate a single clinical event whose symptoms arise following the administration of a single therapy medication. If there are numerous suspect medicines present, this technique evaluates each potential cause independently.

Question	Yes	No	Don't know or not done
Are there previous conclusive reports on this reaction?	+1	0	0
Did the adverse event appear after the suspected drug was given?	+2	−1	0
Did the adverse reaction improve when the drug was discontinued or a specific antagonist was given?	+1	0	0
Did the adverse reaction appear when the drug was readministered?	+2	−1	0
Are there alternative causes that could have caused the reaction?	−1	+2	0
Did the reaction reappear when a placebo was given?	−1	+1	0
Was the drug detected in any body fluid in toxic concentrations?	+1	0	0
Was the reaction more severe when the dose was increased, or less severe when the dose was decreased?	+1	0	0
Did the patient have a similar reaction to the same or similar drugs in any previous exposure?	+1	0	0
Was the adverse event confirmed by any objective evidence?	+1	0	0

Swedish method of causality assessment

The Swedish regulatory agency employed this procedure, which is based on professional judgement. Here, seven elements are used to determine the causality:

i. the order in which the event occurred
ii. information already known about the medicine and its class of pharmaceuticals
iii. dose relationship with the event

iv. drug response pattern from prior drug information
v. dechallenge and rechallenge
vi. alternative candidates such past medical history and current medical problems
vii. concurrent drug use.

The Scores are provided as +1, 0, -1 and the adverse events are classified into four levels 'probable' or 'possible' and 'non-assessable' or 'unlikely'

European ABO System

The European ABO system also categorizes causality into three categories—A, B and O.

A. Sufficient evidences areavailable to assume causal relationship

B.Sufficient information available to accept the possibility of causal relationship
O. Causality is not assessable

Advantages and Limitations

Method	Advantages	Limitations
Naranjo scale	Simple and brief	This method does not explain causality due to interacting drugs.
WHO- UMC scale	Convenient tool for the assessment of individual case reports	Non-probabilistic method and creates extensive unpredictability in evaluation
Probabilistic method	Provide a positive predictive value	Poor specificity and moreover practically complex as they require specifically calculated information data[9]

• 55 •

CHAPTER SEVEN

Labeling Assessment

Overview

Labeling is one of the indispensable part of pharmacovigilance. The adverse events which a patient experiences after taking a suspect medication may or may not be documented. The process of creating a medicine label is cumulative and iterative; it starts with preclinical research and lasts the whole lifespan of the product. A clinician or potential investigator should be able to understand the medicine from the labelled information and decide whether it is suitable to prescribe it or carry out the planned trial based only on the risks and benefits. According to the company's or sponsor's stated protocols, the labelling information should be evaluated every year and updated as appropriate. Depending on the product's level of development and the production of pertinent new information, more frequent modification may be required. The document containing the information about the label is known as reference safety information (RSI). If the adverse event experienced by a patient is well-documented in any of the RSI, then the event is labeled whereas if the event has been experienced for the first time then it is unlabeled. The term listed/labeled is used for the marketed product whereas the term expected or unexpected is used for the products under clinical trial. Different countries have their own labeling documents.

Objective or need of labeling

- The labeling document provides information about the safety and risk profile of the suspected drug in market as well a in clinical trial.
- The document helps the physician to decide whether the drug is suitable for prescribing to a patient or not.
- The document provides information about how to consume the drug.
- Overall, it awares the pharma companies, regulatory authorities as well as the health care profesionals about the safe and effective use of drug.
- A global labelling policy's goal is to make sure that the evaluation of adverse events (AEs) is done consistently and in accordance with worldwide regulatory standards.

Because adverse events (AE) can occur when taking a drug and be caused by excipients, concomitants, treatment medications, any disease, manufacturing concerns, etc., their expectedness is not necessarily a reliable indicator of their causality with the product.

Classification of labeling document:

The labeling documents are known as reference safety information. There are various **RSI** available in different countries.

Investigator Brochure (IB): The clinical and non-clinical information on the investigational product(s) that is known and pertinent to the study of the product is contained in the investigator's brochure (IB), a document. The IB gives information on the justification to investigators and other research participants in order to assist compliance with the major elements of the Protocol, including the dose, frequency, and interval of the dose, administration techniques, and safety monitoring measures. Additionally, it offers background information to aid in the clinical supervision of the study participants.The proposed trial's form, scope, and length should be justified, and there should be enough evidence to assess the trial's potential safety and the necessity of taking extra precautions. The information in the IB has to be updated if any fresh, highly pertinent data is produced throughout the trial. The material provided in the investigator's brochure ought to be succinct, clear, impartial, balanced, and non-promotional in order to enable an unbiased comprehension and to make it easier to determine whether the proposed study is appropriate from a risk-benefit perspective.

SmPC: Every medicine's marketing authorization includes a legal document called the SmPC, or Summary of Product Characteristics. For medical practitioners, the publication serves as a foundation for knowledge on the usage of medications. The SmPC's information is updated frequently to reflect the release of new information.

CCDS: The marketing authorization holder (MAH)/pharmaceutical company's internal document known as the Company Core Data Sheet (CCDS) or Core Data Sheet (CDS) outlines the company's viewpoint on the safety profile of any medicine. The CCDS acts as the foundation for medicine prescriptions as well as for international advertising and promotional initiatives. First and foremost, a CCDS is needed to ensure that all drug products are labelled uniformly around the world and to provide Reference Safety Information for evaluating the product's aggregate reports .

USPI: The USPI outlines the prescribed prescription consumption. It is an integral aspect of the application for marketing authorization of a new drug or medicine in the United States and includes information on usage for healthcare professionals.The USPI is divided into the Table of Contents, the Full Prescribing Information (FPI), and the Highlights of Prescribing Information. Patient Information is frequently included after the USPI. A separate document is offered if the product has a medication guide. Each section of the USPI adheres to a defined framework to give healthcare practitioners uniform, up-to-date drug information.The highlights of prescribing information contains dosage forms, contraindications, warning and precautions, adverse reactions, drug interaction, use in specific population in brief. The full prescribing information contains detail on indication and usage, dosage and administration, dosage form and strength, contraindications, warning and precautions, adverse reactions, drug interactions, use in specific populations, drug abuse and dependence, overdosage, description, clinical pharmacology, non-clinical toxilogy, clinical studies, references, how supplied/storage and handling, patient counelling information.

Canadian monograph: A Product Monograph is a factual, scientific report on a drug product that, free of promotional material, describes the drug's properties, claims, indications, and usage guidelines. It also includes any additional information that might be necessary for the drug to be used in the best, safest possible way.There are three sections in monograph:Health Professional Information; Scientific Information; andPatient Medication Information (PMI). The name of the drug, its therapeutic or pharmacologic classification, its effects and/or clinical pharmacology, and its indications should all be appropriately described in a product monograph. The Product Monograph should also include the following information: warnings, precautions, adverse reactions, drug interactions, effects on laboratory tests, storage and stability, special handling instructions, pharmaceutical information, information on clinical trials, microbiology, toxicology, and information for patients. It should also include information on contraindications, dosage and administration, overdose symptoms and treatment, dosage forms, warnings, and precautions. The Product Monograph must also provide the dates of the first approval and, if appropriate, the most recent amendment.

To determine whether an event is expected or not is a two step process; the first is to check whether the event (including its synonym) is in RSI or not and next to determine if the nature, severity, specificity and outcome of the event in question is in accordance with the previous observations or not.

Nature, Severity, Specificity, Outcome

Nature
An event which is chronic than one existing in the labeling document should be considered as unexpected. For example: chronic hepatitis is considered to be unexpected when labeling document states acute hepatitis.

Severity
An event which is more severe than one existing in the labeling document should be considered as unexpected. Example: Fluminant hepatitis is considered to be unexpected when labeling document states only hepatitis.

Specificity
An event which is more specific than described in the labeling document should be considered unexpected.

Outcome
An event with outcome of fatal should always be considered as unexpected unless it is clearly written in the monograph that the event may cause death.

CHAPTER EIGHT

Medical coding

A code is a method for converting a piece of information (for example, a letter, word, phrase, or gesture) into another form or representation (one sign into another sign), not necessarily of the same type.

Auto Coding: The medical term recorded by the investigator gets coded automatically if it exactly matches with the appropriate term available in the medical dictionary.

Manual Coding: The auto coding fails for the terms (called as verbatim) which do not match exactly with the appropriate level of hierarchy in the medical dictionary. All these terms are manually coded by a qualified person called as coder. The medical coder will find the appropriate match for the term by browsing the assigned dictionary and will manually code it.

<u>Different coding dictionaries</u>

Dictionary	Version update
MedDRA	Twice a year – In March and September
WHODD	Quarterly – In March, June, September and December
WHO-ART	Quarterly

COSTART - Coding Symbols for Thesaurus of Adverse Reaction Terms

ICD 10 CM - International Classification of Diseases, Tenth Revision, Clinical Modification

MedDRA - Medical Dictionary for Regulatory Activities

WHO-ART - World Health Organization Adverse Reactions Terminology

WHO-DD - World Health Organization Drug Dictionary

The **Certified MedDRA Coder (CMC)** examination is an online assessment of one's knowledge of MedDRA coding and of the MedDRATerm Selection: Points to Consider (PTC) document. The CMC examination includes short verbatim questions requiring single answers and narrative questions from which various data (e.g., medical history, indication, events, etc.) can be coded.

MedDRA (Medical Dictionary for Regulatory Activities) is a clinically-validated international medical terminology used by regulatory authorities and the regulated biopharmaceutical industry. It was developed by ICH and MSSO (Maintenance and Support Services Organization) is responsible for the maintenance.

Medical conditions Indications Investigations (tests, results) Medical and surgical procedures Medical, social, family history Medication errors Product quality issues Device-related issues Product use issues Pharmacogenetic terms Toxicologic issues are under the scope of MedDRA.

Patient demographics, drug information, frequency, numerical results, severity descriptors are out of scope of Meddra.

Updates- March and September every year, current version 25.1 in March it would be 26.0. Updates of march is major update where all the levels are modified whereas in august only PT and LLTs are altered.

MedDRA is widely used in Clinical Study Reports, Investigators' Brochures, Core Company Safety Information, Marketing Applications, Publications, Prescribing Information , Advertising, Individual case safety reports.

Hierarchy with Example

System Organ Class (SOC) (27)	Infections and infestations
High Level Group Term (HLGT) (337)	Viral infectious disorders
High Level Term (HLT) (1737)	Influenza viral infections
Preferred Term (PT) (25,412)	Influenza
Lowest Level Term (LLT) (85,091)	Flu

Each MedDRA term is assigned an 8-digit numeric code which is Non-expressive. Fever (10016558)

Each medical concept is associated with a particular SOC but sometimes there can be multiple SOC to represent one single concept. This is known as multi-axial terminology.

For example influenza is an infection as well as respiratory, thoracic and mediastinal disorders. So both the SOCs are correct but for the sake of standardization and prevention of double counting, a primary SOC is selected, in this case the primary SOC is infection.

Coding conventions

- Do Not Alter MedDRA: MedDRA structure cannot be altered, alteration of primary SOC is not acceptable.

ReportedLLTSelected
Lip sore Lip sore (PT Lip pain)
Lip sores Sores lip (PT Cheilitis)

- Always Select a Lowest Level Term that most accurately reflects the reported verbatim information. A single letter difference in a reported verbatim text can impact the meaning of the word and consequently the term selection
- Select Only Current Lowest Level Terms
- Use of Medical Judgment in Term Selection when exact term is unavailable.
- In some cases, it may be appropriate to select more than one MedDRA LLT to represent the reported information. If only one term is selected, specificity may be lost. Example There is no single MedDRA term for "metastatic gingival cancer". Therefore, the options are to Select LLT **Gingival cancer** OR LLT **Metastatic carcinoma**
- <u>**Conflicting/Ambiguous/Vague Information** :</u> Attempt to obtain more specific information, clarification attempt. If not possible, use conservative approach.

Example: GU pain (GU can be genito-urinary or gastric ulcer). If no reply is received, code with pain.

Turned blue (vague term, could be a person or even product)

Hyperkalaemia with a serum potassium of 1.6 mEq/L (contradictory, code to **serum potassium abnormal**)

- <u>**Combination Terms :**</u>

Hypertensive cardiomegaly, Diabetic retinopathy

If a diagnosis and its characteristic signs or symptoms are reported, select a term for the diagnosis.

- <u>**Age specific codes**</u>

Example: Developed psychosis at age 6 years = childhood psychosis

- <u>**Results of investigations as ARs/Aes**</u>

Example: Glucose 40 mg/dL= Glucose low (as Glucose is clearly below the standard range)

Glucose was 40= Glucose abnormal (ambiguous information as no unit is there, clarify)

- Surgery, hospitalization, death are outcomes. If these are included with any AR/AE then only the associated event should be coded.

Example: Death due to myocardial infarction= Myocardial infarction.

Patient was found dead = Found death (since cause unknown).

<u>Problems faced while coding</u>

- Spelling mistakes
- Illegible verbatim terms
- Use of abbreviations with multiple meaning
- Multiple medical concepts in a single verbatim
- Use of vague, conflicting, ambiguous verbatim terms.
- Diagnosis and signs/symptoms in same verbatim.
- Event is recorded without mentioning the site e.g. ulcer is recorded without additional information like mouth ulcer, leg ulcer etc.
- Too much of unnecessary information in verbatim.
- Wrong information in verbatim.
- Clarification query not raised when required.
- Multiple Product names recorded together as a single term.
- The coding conventions are not fixed, companies can alter the conventions based upon their regulatory or customer requirement.

CHAPTER NINE

Narrative Writing

Overview

Narrative is a document required by the regulatory agencies of different countries. Because it gives a thorough account of an adverse event report, narrative writing is regarded as the core of the case processing procedure. The narrative often highlights the whole array of data needed to evaluate an individual case safety report as a whole. A "narrative" is, by definition, any description of related events that is presented to the reader in a logical order.It details everything a patient has gone through after ingesting or receiving a suspected drug.It is a stand-alone medical report of the negative effects or reactions that a patient had at a particular period.It is a narrative that details the entire clinical progression of an adverse event or response. A narrative is a part of IND, clinical trial reports, DSUR, PBRER. The narrative summarizes patient characteristics, therapy details, events experienced, outcomes, lab data, causality in a logical sequence. Usually narrative is written for serious cases

Purpose:

To offer a succinct description of identified/specific adverse events (AES) that occur in a patient in order to establish a causal link between the medicine and the occurrence.

Objective: The narrative's goal is to present all relevant clinical and associated information, such as patient characteristics, therapeutic details, past medical history, clinical course of the event(s), laboratory data, and any other material that supports or rejects an ADR diagnosis. The data should be presented in a sensible time order.

<u>Regulatory Perspectives:</u>

Company narratives are required for all significant reactions, according to the ICH regulation (E2B) on data components and criteria for electronic reporting of individual ADR cases.

Narratives are supposed to be produced for all cases reported promptly to any regulatory authority, but they are also helpful and should be made available for other sorts of reports and purposes.

<u>Content of narrative</u>

- Report source and its type
- Day 0 or IRD
- Patient details (age, sex, race etc but not initials)
- Suspected drug, concomitant medication, past drugs, treatment drugs taken
- Dose, frequency, route of administration of drug
- Relevant medical history, current conditions
- Allergy details
- Events experienced in the form of verbatim
- Date and time of event onset
- Autopsy detail in case of death cases.
- Event outcome
- Relevant laboratory tests and diagnosis
- Seriousness of the events (hospitalization, conginetal anomaly, permanent disability or medically significant)
- Action taken with the suspected drug, dechallenge and rechallenge information
- Causality assessment (both reporter and MAH causality)
- Investigetor or Sponsor opinion on causality
- Follow-up details

Method of writing

Abbreviations: Narrative should be free of abbreviations and acronyms, short forms should not be used while writing a narrative.

Special characters: Special characters should not be used while writing narratives.

Grammar and spelling: Care must be taken to ensure that the grammatical and spelling errors do not occur. Spel checker can be used for this purpose. Alternatively, the narrative can be written in MS word document as it heps to identify such errors.

Use of parenthesis or quotes: Parenthesis or quotes can be used if any text is copied from the source document.

Dash, hypens or spacing: Dash or hypens can be used but spacing should be uniform. Use the justify alignment in MS word to prevent spacing errors.

Patient details: Patient's name or initials should not be used anywhere in the narrative. Gender, age, ethnicity or other demographics can be used.

Date and time: Date and time format should be same throughout the narrative. Stament like four days ago, 3 weeks later should be avoided.

Drug name: Drug name should be generic.

Futuristic statement: Futuristic statement should not be written in narrative.

Sources of information

Medwatch form
   CIOMS form
   Literature reports
   Email communication
   Telephonic contacts
   Medical or hospital records (including discharge summary)
   Various ICSR reports

Social media like lay press, internet.
Reports from regulatory authorities
Data classification forms

Points to remember while writing narrative

- Narrative should always be written in past tense.
- Chronology of the narrative should be maintained throughout the narrative.
- Language and style should be in accordance with the SOP.
- Futuristic information or future tense should not be used whiling writing narrative.
- Short and succinct sentences should be used. The message must be concise and unambiguous.
- Do not copy and paste the narrative from the ICSR form directly.
- Grammar and spelling should be thoroughly verified.
- Reporter's name, contact details should never be disclosed in narrative.
- Patient's name and initials, identification number, social security number should not be written in narrative.
- The meaning of the narrative should not be changed by adding own words.
- Short forms should be avoided but globally accepted abbreviations can be used (like COVID, UTI, EEG).

<u>Example of narrative</u>

Spontaneous case received from a 31 year old male patient with the events of diarrhea, vomiting using ABC injection. The patient had a relevant medical history of abdominal pain.

In Aug-2022, the patient started on ABC injection every three weeks for treatment of Rheumatoid arthritis. In Sep-2022, the patient experienced diarrhea, vomiting. After consulting with his physician, the patient discontinued the drug in Sep-2022.

At the time of the report, the outcome of events, diarrhea and vomiting were not recovered. This case has been assessed as medically not confirmed, non-serious, and unlabeled as per the prescribing information of the product.

CHAPTER TEN

Individual Case Safety Report (ICSR) Processing

A step in the pharmacovigilance process is the ICSR process.

A suspected adverse reaction to a medication that occurs in a single patient at a specific time is reported individually using the format and content known as an Individual Case Safety Report (ICSR). The GVP Guidelines

A legitimate ICSR should have an identified reporter, an identifiable patient, an adverse response, and a suspicious pharmaceutical product.

Who all are involves in ICSR Process?

The following stakeholders involves in ICSR Process

1. Safety Data Entry associate (SDEA)
2. Case Processor (CP)
3. Quality Reviewer (QR)
4. Medical Reviewer (MR)

Adverse event reports must be translated from the native tongue into English by a translator.

When processing cases, ICSR stakeholders should keep the following in mind:

• Enter data exactly as supplied by the reporter;

• Avoid translating data from local languages into English; and

• Avoid making any interpretations or assumptions.

<u>ICSR Process</u>

The following steps involves in ICSR Process

1. Case Intake/Receipt
2. Triage
3. Data entry and Case Processing
4. Quality Review
5. Medical Review
6. Distribution/Regulatory submission

Every business keeps its own Pharmacovigilance safety database, as we covered in our previous piece "Pharmacovigilance Process."

What is a safety database?

The Safety Data Base is where all ICSRs for a company's drug(s) that have been gathered from all around the world are centralised.

It is critical that any safety database be maintained with the latest regulatory requirements and validated to meet international standards and business requirements.

Some of the industry-wide safety databases are available here.

1. Argus
2. ARISg/LifeSphere Safety
3. PV Works
4. Safety Easy
5. SafetyBase Interchange

Safety databases should adhere to 21 CFR part 11 in order to be in compliance with Good Pharmacovigilance Practice.

All actions and decisions done during the ICSR process are documented inside the safety database.

ICSR Process Step 1: Case Intake/Receipt

• Equipment like email or fax used to receive source papers (adverse event reports)

• SDEA monitors at least once per working day.

• SDEA receives reports in a variety of media, such as paper or computer format, but not just.

• Determining case validity - Only cases that meet regulatory reporting requirements are legitimate.

• Identify the type of case (solicited and unsolicited report types)

• Translate into English country-specific adverse event reports
If further medical data is required, request it.

• Prior to the entry of an ICSR, SDEA runs a duplicate check-in of safety databases.

• The database will be searched to determine whether the case is a new initial case—that is, one that has never been entered into the database before—or whether it relates to a case that has already been received.

ICSR Process Step 2: Triage

Triage is the process of reviewing, ranking, and prioritising collected safety information as well as recording just the necessary details in order to swiftly and accurately determine which cases require expedited reporting.

All reported Adverse Events, unique circumstances, and Product Complaints connected to Adverse Events are subject to triage, regardless of whether the report type is solicited or uninvited. As a result, it aids in sorting ICSRs in the safety database and assigning them to the appropriate regulatory reporting division for submission.

In triage, two different processes are involves,

- Triage of any fresh ICSR data received, and
- Secondly the medical assessment (Medical triage)

SDEA is in charge of triaging cases for an initial examination
• Assessing the case's legitimacy (valid or non-valid case)
• the seriousness of each adverse event is evaluated.
• Identifying a questionable product from a corporation
• evaluation of listedness and causation. case priority in accordance with the regulations
Medical triage is done by a medical reviewer.
. Both requested and unrequested post-marketing situations necessitate a medical triage.
• A thorough evaluation of the gravity of each adverse event

• A thorough evaluation of the causation and listedness for any association between a suspicious product and an adverse event

• Determining if the occurrence is regarded as a monitoring gap

ICSR Process Step 3: Data entry and Case Processing

Case processors carry out the following tasks.

• Assessing the case's legitimacy (valid or non-valid case)

• A duplicate check is conducted

• List the case's sources.

• Entering data from safety database reports of adverse events. Update patient and reporter information in the safety database.

• Enters medical history and test results that the reporter provides.

• Coding of medications identified by the reporter as suspect or concurrent, and updating dose, treatment dates, and action taken for suspect medications

• Enters information about all reported reactions incl. MedDRA coding, start/stop dates,

• Adverse event data and coding using MedDRA

• Seriousness assessment

• Labelling and Causality assessment

• Assessment of dechallenge and rechallenge

• Event ranking in the safety database

• Narrative writing · query creation to obtain additional information, case clarification, and additional details.

The case processor routes the case to the quality assessment step after data entry.

ICSR Process Step 4: Quality Review

• A quality reviewer will conduct a quality analysis of the case to guarantee that adverse event reports are processed and entered with accuracy and consistency.

• A quality reviewer verifies the authenticity of the cases, the choice and coding of the event terms, the coding of questionable goods, and the general coherence of the data.

• The follow-up information's medical significance is also determined by the quality reviewer.

• A quality reviewer determines if an incident should be listed, examines and validates the seriousness, and completes or adjusts the narrative as appropriate.

ICSR Process Step 5: Medical Review

The first-level phase in signal detecting activities is physician review, which is carried out by a safety physician (medical reviewer).

• A medical review examines the entire case evaluation and the accuracy of the data, including validation of the judgement of listedness.

• The medical reviewer completes the SUSAR procedure as necessary and performs the company's causality assessment, clinical evaluation remark, and analysis.

• The final decision on seriousness assessment rests with the medical reviewer.

• The case is examined from a medical standpoint to ensure that it is accurate, comprehensive, and consistent.

• MedDRA narratives and coding are examined from a medical standpoint

• Verify sources of information if a doctor deems it essential.

• With the exception of spontaneous non-serious listed and solicited non-serious listed ICSRs, medical reviewers offer pharmacovigilance commentary.

ICSR Process Step 6: Distribution/Regulatory submission

After a medical review, cases are sent for distribution, which entails submitting an ICSR to regulatory authorities. The safety database is set up to automatically schedule and generate both expedited and non-expedited reports, and the safety data entry associate is in charge of regularly checking the database worklist reports to ensure appropriate and timely submissions

list of pharmacovigilance companies in India

Pharmacovigilance Companies In Mumbai

- 1. Apotex
- 2. Alembic
- 3. Colgate Palmolive
- 4. Sun Pharma
- 5. Siroclina Pharm
- 6. TCS
- 7. Cognizant
- 8. IQVIA
- 9. PVCON
- 10. Nucleon Therapeutics
- 11. ADVANZ Pharma
- 12. Brill Pharma
- 13. Piramal Enterprises
- 14. Ipca Laboratories
- 15. Clini Excel Lifesciences
- 16. Glenmark
- 17. Covance
- 18. Wockhardt
- 19. Macleods
- 20. Rhyme LifeSciences
- 21. Cipla

- 22. Genesis Pharmaceuticals
- 23. Flamingo Pharma
- 24. Reliance Life Sciences
- 25. MedVigil
- 26. Bayer
- 27. Lupin
- 28. Concordia International
- 29. Unichem Laboratories
- 30. USV Private
- 31. Abbott
- 32. Elc-Group
- 33. J & J
- 34. Spectrum Pharmaceuticals
- 35. Sanofi
-

Pharmacovigilance Companies In Ahmedabad

- 1. Karmic Lifesciences
- 2. Cliantha Research
- 3. Apcer Life Sciences
- 4. COD Research
- 5. Lambda
- 6. Torrent Pharma
- 7. Otsuka Pharmaceuticals
- 8. Zydus Cadila
- 9. Veeda Clinical Research
- 10. Arkus Research
- 11. Ethicare-cro

Pharmacovigilance Companies In Delhi

- 1. APCER Life sciences
- 2. Kinapse
- 3. Baxter

- 4. Clinfomatrix
- 5. Awinsa Life Sciences (Gurgaon)
- 6. Fresenius Kabi
- 7. Symogen
- 8. Jubilant Life sciences
- 9. Wipro (Noida)
- 10. APC Pharma
- 11. Syneos Health
- 12. MSD Merck
- 13. SunPharma
- 14. DDreg
- 15. Elite safety, Gurugaon
- 16. Pharmalex
- 17. Pharmxl
- 18. Johnson Johnson

Pharmacovigilance Companies in Pune

- 1. Covance
- 2. TCS
- 3. Cognizant
- 4. Eversana
- 5. Springer Nature Group
- 6. Syneos Health
- 7. EduceSolutions

Pharmacovigilance Companies in Bangalore

- 1. Iqvia
- 2. Biocon
- 3. Accenture
- 4. AstraZeneca
- 5. Bluefish Pharmaceuticals
- 6. Covance
- 7. StridesAcrolabs

- 8. MMSHoldings
- 9. Norwich Clinical Services
- 10. Kinapse
- 11. 4C Pharma
- 12. Microlabs
- 13. Novo Nordisk
- 14. Qvigilance (Formely Quanticate)
- 15. DZS Clinical Services
- 16. Pharmaleaf
- 17. FMD K&L (Merged with iMed Global)
- 18. Navitas Life Sciences
- 19. Mylan
- 20. Astalynx Global
- 21. Shilpamedicare
- 22. Cognizant
- 23. WDB MD
- 24. GSK
- 25. Deloitte (Consulting)
- 26. Voisin Consulting Services
- 27. Indegene
- 28. Alcon
- 29. Eli Lilly
- 30. Medreich
- 31. Elanco
- 32. Parexel
- 33. Novotech
- 34. Augur Safety Services
- 35. Pharmed
- 36. GSS Pharma

Pharmacovigilance Companies in Hyderabad

- 1. Novartis
- 2. Paraxel
- 3. Makrocare

- 4. Mahindra Satyambsg
- 5. Dr Reddy's
- 6. Aurobindo
- 7. Sristek
- 8. Shantha Biotechnics
- 9. Nektar Therapeutics
- 10. Vimta Labs
- 11. Biological E. Ltd
- 12. Medhimalayas
- 13. Sri Krishna Pharma
- 14. Laurus Labs
- 15. Santha Biotech
- 16. Piramal
- 17. Genpact
- 18. Inventive
- 19.Granules

Pharmacovigilance Companies in Chennai

- ICON
- Accenture
- Rx Md
- Take Solutions
- TCS
- Cognizant
- Emcure
- Inventive
- I3
- Iplex

CHAPTER TWELVE

Special Notes For Interview

What is Pharmacovigilance?

Pharmacovigilance is the science relating to the detection, assessment, understanding and prevention of adverse effects or any other drug-related problem, with a view to identifying information about potential new hazards and preventing harm to patients.

Significance or objective of Pharmacovigilance?

• The collection of better data on medicines and their safety

• Rapid and robust assessment of issues relating to the safety of medicines

• Effective regulatory action to deliver safe and effective use of medicines

• Empowerment of patients through reporting and participation

• Increased levels of transparency and better communication

What is Adverse Event?

Any untoward medical occurrence in a patient or clinical investigation subject administered a pharmaceutical product, and which does not necessarily have to have a causal relationship with this treatment or Any unfavorable and unintended sign (including an abnormal laboratory finding, for example), symptom, or disease temporally associated with the use of a medicinal product, whether or not considered related to the medicinal product.

What is Adverse Drug Reaction (ADR)?

A response to a medicinal product which is noxious and unintended. This includes adverse reactions which arise from use within and outside the terms of the marketing authorisation (overdose, off-label use, misuse, abuse and medication errors) Occupational exposure.

•Response to a medicinal product" means that a causal relationship between a medicinal product and an adverse event is at least a reasonable possibility

•Implied relationship" – spontaneous reports of adverse events/ experiences where the causal relationship is unknown/unstated should still be reported.

Many interviewer will try to confuse you by asking question about Difference between ADR and AE. In short it's all about causal relationship with the drug . Also keep in mind about the difference between side effect and adverse effect.

In my previous poster upload you must have read about ICSR, if not please check out. So I will not discuss much about ICSR, but will give you general idea about its validation, source and timelines.

<u>So what are the Minimum Criteria for Safety Report or ICSR to be valid</u>

1. Identifiable patient
2. Identifiable substance/medicinal product
3. One or more suspected adverse reaction or event
4. Identifiable reporter

When we say identifiable patient, what it refers, It refers the patient identity such as name, age, date of birth, gender and even age group (neonate, infant, adolescent, adult and elderly) is also an identification.

Same goes for reporter, his/her qualification, Profession or email id, address, phone number through which we can identify them

<u>Seriousness Criteria for ICSR Reports</u>

There are some events which investigator, marketing authorisation holder or company consider serious also called medically significant events and these are listed in IME (Important medical event) list. Apart from those event or even those if cause any of the below outcome will be considered as serious.

Suppose patient took drug which resulted in pneumonia which requires hospitalisation. Now here company IME list will consider pneumonia as serious and also it lead to hospitalisation, so we consider 2 seriousness criteria i.e, Hospitalisation and Medically significant.

- Death
- Event was considered life-threatening
- Incapacity
- Disability
- Congenital anomaly
- Hospitalisation
- Patient is already admitted but prolongation of hospitalisation is required- Here interviewer can try to trick by asking how long stay in hospital is considered as prolongation and answer is more than 24 hours.
- Event Preferred MedDRA term appears in the IME (Important Medical Event) listing
- Event considered to be of "medical significance" by the reporter (HCP/ Investigator)

<u>Timelines</u>

Various manufacturers have set their own timelines to avoid any late cases. Timelines changes from one drug to another and also on basis of causality and seriousness.

The most common timelines

- **Death/Life-threatening** cases: 7 days
- **Other** seriousness criteria: 15 days
- **Non-serious**: 90 days

<u>Day Zero</u>

The first date on which any representative of an organisation was first notified of the minimum essential elements for expedited reporting. This date also implies in when any of the company partner/ vendor receive the report.

Day of Receipt

The day of receipt is the date on which company/ manufacturer was provided with an AE report/ADR report.

What is GVP?

Good Pharmacovigilance Practices (GVP) are a set of measures drawn up to facilitate the performance of pharmacovigilance in the European Union (EU). GVP apply to marketing-authorisation holders, the European Medicines Agency (EMA) and medicines regulatory authorities in EU Member States. They cover medicines authorised centrally via the Agency as well as medicines authorised at national level.

What are the modules associated with GVP

- Module I – Pharmacovigilance systems and their quality systems
- Module II – Pharmacovigilance system master file
- Module III – Pharmacovigilance inspections
- Module IV – Pharmacovigilance audits
- Module V – Risk management systems
- Module VI – Collection, management and submission of reports of suspected adverse reactions to medicinal products
- Module VII – Periodic safety update report
- Module VIII – Post-authorisation safety studies
- Module IX – Signal management
- Module X – Additional monitoring
- Module XV – Safety communication

What are the Different forms of reporting an ADR/AE?

- CIOMS- (Council for International Organization of Medical Sciences). It is used globally.
- US- Med Watch (Form 3500)
- UK – Yellow Card iv.
- Australia- Blue Card
- India- SARRF (Suspected Adverse Reaction Reporting Form)

What is SUSAR (Suspected Un Expected Serious Adverse Reaction)?

Serious cases can be seen only in clinical trial reports but not in solicited and spontaneous reports. It should be from clinical trial report, would be serious, it is unexpected, and the reports were not found in IB the causality should be possible.

Name the regulatory bodies in USA, UK, Japan and India?

- USA: United States Food and drug administration (USFDA).
- UK: Medicines and Healthcare Product Regulatory Authority (MHRA)
- Japan: Ministry of Health, Labour and Welfare (MHLW).
- India: Central Drugs Standard Control Organization (CDSCO)
- Canada: Health Canada
- Australia: Therapeutics Good Administration (TGA)
- China: State Food and Drug Administration
- Europe: Europe Medicine Agency (EMA)
- France: AFSSAPS

<u>Listedness/ Unlistedness:</u>

Any reaction which is not included in the Company Core Safety Information within a company's core data sheet for a marketed product is called unlisted. If it is included, it is termed listed.

<u>Expectedness:</u>

Expectedness refers to the AE whether serious or being previously observed and documented in Reference Safety Information (i.e. IB, SmPC, Package Insert, CCSI).

<u>Unexpectedness:</u>

Unexpectedness refers to AE not being observed or documented in the Reference Safety Information (i.e. IB, SmPC, Package Insert, CCSI).

<u>Action Taken:</u>

It refers to the action taken to suspect drug with that of an event. The possible actions taken to the drug is:

i. Drug withdrawal/ Drug Discontinuation

ii. Dose not change

iii. Dose increases

iv. Dose decreases

v. Unknown i.e. we do not know about the action taken.

Dechallenge / Re challenge:

They both are applicable when the drug is discontinued due to an AE.

Dechallenge:

The withdrawal of a drug from a patient; the point at which the continuity, reduction or disappearance of adverse effects may be observed. When the Event is Resolved, it is known as Positive Dechallenge When the event is not resolved, it is known as Negative Dechallenge.

Re challenge:

The point at which a drug is again given to a patient after its previous withdrawal. It is applicable only when there is Positive Dechallenge. When the Event is reoccurred, it is known as Positive Re challenge, and when the event not occurred it is known as Negative Re challenge.